Praise for *Pitch Perfect*

"Great advice on pitching bloggers. Get it now, devs."

—Steve Streza, Lead Platform Developer, *Pocket*

"A must-read for anyone trying to get their app reviewed by the media."

—Aaron Watkins, President, *Appency PR*

"*Pitch Perfect* should be required reading for anyone who is trying to understand the ins and outs of getting press coverage for your app."

—Brian Akaka, Founder, *Appular Mobile App PR*

"As a long-time indie app publisher, I felt like someone had finally lifted the veil over what really goes on in the minds of the reviewers at a major blog site."

—Ken Landau, Co-Founder, *mobileAge, LLC*

"This book is fabulous. I wish I would have read it three weeks ago. It would have saved me some embarrassment. I haven't been able to put it down since I started."

—Jon Fawcett, Owner, *[Fuse]Chicken*

"As someone who works in app PR on the other side of the fence, *Pitch Perfect* gives a fascinating insight into the world of bloggers I'm looking to excite!"

—Rob Shoesmith, Marketing & PR Executive, *MEDL Mobile*

"There are tons of great mobile-programming resources, but very few great resources for app marketing. Erica and Steve do a fantastic job in their book *Pitch Perfect* explaining in detail the best way to raise awareness for your indie apps. I have virtual yellow highlighter all over my copy!"

—Elia Freedman, CEO, *Infinity Softworks*, Maker of powerOne Calculators

"Before iMore, I worked for over a decade in marketing, and I can't stress enough how important it is, and how often developers and manufacturers either forget to do it or simply do it dead wrong. If you're a developer or a manufacturer, especially and independent or a kickstarter, do yourself—and us bloggers—a favor and check out *Pitch Perfect*."

—Rene Ritchie, Editor-in-Chief, *iMore*

"This book illustrates the intricate relationship between product developers and bloggers so well that I can almost hear David Attenborough's disembodied voice narrating the complex dance."

—Carl E. Moebis @ *iBackFlip Studios LLC*

Pitch Perfect

The Art of Promoting Your App on the Web

Erica Sadun · Steve Sande

♦♦Addison-Wesley

Upper Saddle River, NJ • Boston • Indianapolis • San Francisco
New York • Toronto • Montreal • London • Munich • Paris • Madrid

The publisher offers excellent discounts on this book when ordered in quantity for bulk purchases or special sales, which may include electronic versions and/or custom covers and content particular to your business, training goals, marketing focus, and branding interests. For more information, please contact:

U.S. Corporate and Government Sales
1-800-382-3419
corpsales@pearsontechgroup.com

For sales outside of the U.S., please contact:

International Sales
international@pearsoned.com

Visit us on the Web: informit.com/aw

The Library of Congress cataloging-in-publication data is on file.

Copyright © 2013 Erica Sadun and Steve Sande

ISBN-13: 978-0-321-91761-4
ISBN-10: 0-321-91761-8

Text printed in the United States on recycled paper at R.R. Donnelley in Crawfordsville, Indiana.

First printing: May 2013

Editor-in-Chief
Mark Taub

Senior Acquisitions Editor
Trina MacDonald

Senior Development Editor
Chris Zahn

Managing Editor
Kristy Hart

Senior Project Editor
Jovana San Nicolas-Shirley

Copy Editor
Sheri Replin

Indexer
Cheryl Lenser

Proofreaders
Sarah Kearns
Jennifer Gallant

Editorial Assistant
Olivia Basegio

Cover Designer
Chuti Prasertsith

Senior Compositor
Gloria Schurick

❖

This book is dedicated to all of our fellow bloggers at TUAW, with a hearty wefwef and a hug. You are our attract point because we certainly aren't blogging for the money! With warm thoughts and good wishes, we $opportunity_name_alt this for you.

❖

Contents at a Glance

Table of Contents

Acknowledgments

Thanks to everyone at TUAW for all of their support and to all the readers and friends who helped with suggestions and feedback. Special thanks go out to advance readers Zane Revai, Mike Kale, Colin Cox, Robert Jen, Greg Hartstein, TJ Luoma, Maurice Sharp, Kelly Guimont, Michael Jones, David Caolo, and everyone else who pitched in with early feedback and help.

Thanks also to all the people who allowed us to quote them, use their pitches, and interview them as part of developing this book. Special thanks to Melissa Davis for her above-the-call-of-duty feedback and insights.

Thank you to our spouses, for being there, for supporting us, and for being wonderful people. We appreciate you more than we can say.

Finally, we thank Trina MacDonald and the Pearson team who helped transition this book from a little indie-pub-that-could to the polished traditional book you now hold in your hands.

About the Authors

Erica Sadun (@ericasadun) writes lots of books and blogs at TUAW. When not writing, she's a full-time parent of geeks who are brushing up on their world-domination skills. According to her academic dosimeter, she's acquired more education than any self-respecting person might consider wise. She enjoys deep-diving into technology and has written, co-written, and contributed to dozens of books about computing and digital media. Sadun has also blogged at Ars Technica, O'Reilly, and Lifehacker.

Steve Sande (@stevensande) is considering an intervention to heal his addiction to writing. He's the Hardware Editor at TUAW and has written millions of words for the blog. Steve has authored numerous books for Que, Take Control Books, and Apress, is married to a rocket scientist, and spends his days being bossed around by a cat. His gray beard and baseball cap can be seen every Wednesday afternoon at 5 PM ET on TUAW TV Live (http://www.tuaw.com/tag/tuawtvlive).

Sadun and Sande are the founders of Sand Dune Books and co-authors of the best-selling *Talking to Siri: Learning the Language of Apple's Intelligent Assistant*.

We Want to Hear from You!

As the reader of this book, you are our most important critic and commentator. We value your opinion and want to know what we're doing right, what we could do better, what areas you'd like to see us publish in, and any other words of wisdom you're willing to pass our way.

You can email or write me directly to let us know what you did or didn't like about this book—as well as what we can do to make our books stronger.

Please note that we cannot help you with technical problems related to the topic of this book, and that due to the high volume of mail we receive, we might not be able to reply to every message.

When you write, be sure to include this book's title and author as well as your name and phone or email address.

Email: trina.macdonald@pearson.com

Mail: Reader Feedback
Addison-Wesley Professional
800 East 96th Street
Indianapolis, IN 46240 USA

Reader Services

Visit our website and register this book at **informit.com/register** for convenient access to any updates, downloads, or errata that might be available for this book.

Foreword

When the App Store debuted, there was the inevitable gold rush toward this nascent smartphone app market, which Apple helped make more accessible to everyday developers. As time goes on, developers can no longer rely on being familiar with code alone to sell their hard work online. As usual, if you are a small shop, you have to wear many hats. The marketing hat is not a comfortable one for many developers, but it's critical to getting your message to your customers.

Erica and Steve have just about seen it all when it comes to marketing. While blogging at TUAW (The Unofficial Apple Weblog), they have received hundreds, if not thousands, of press releases, personal pitches, and offbeat marketing ploys. Over time, they've synthesized what they've seen work and what they've seen fail, and what they've come up with is in this book.

I think you'll find the advice in this book useful if you're out there alone, trying to send your app into the world. By using this book, you'll pay careful attention to the pitch you craft to tell your own app's story—and with a little luck, you'll find success on the App Store.

—**Victor Agreda, Jr.**, Editor-in-Chief, TUAW.com

Preface

You just spent months developing your product. So, why are you spending less than ten minutes promoting it?

Reviews from popular websites can make or break you. Having your product featured on a top website in a positive light turns sales from lackluster to blockbuster. Some entrepreneurs work on their apps and hardware to the point of exhaustion, spending insane hours building, testing, and tweaking. Then, they send in weak, quickly written pitches that fail to sell their excitement and showcase the fruit of their efforts. These two-minute emails and months-in-development ideas quickly move from a blogger's inbox to the trashcan rather than getting featured on the front page of a site.

Who This Book Is For

This book is for anyone who's spent months sweating to create a product, whether building an app or bringing a tech-hardware product to market. You've expended all that effort to perfect your wares; now, take the time to learn how to market it effectively. If you have an app or device that you're planning to bring to market, this is the book you need to read.

This book offers simple and practical advice with real-world examples. The topics discussed help you strengthen the way you think about promotion and marketing. You'll see where other developers have gone wrong and where they've gotten it exactly right, lessons that you can apply to your own marketing.

In this book, you learn from experts and noted bloggers Steve Sande and Erica Sadun about the successful pitch. You discover how to effectively position your product, build relationships with blogs and bloggers, and sell your product's story. Although you won't be guaranteed positive reviews, you do learn how to avoid many of the most common pitfalls that send your message off-track.

Why Pitch Perfect

Chances are pretty good that independent developers who are just starting out don't have deep pockets for a beautifully orchestrated marketing campaign. They need to be extremely clever about getting the word out to the public in the most cost-effective way possible.

Developers, both software and hardware, need bloggers to help promote their efforts and broadcast new releases and updates. Bloggers need product developers because without a topic to write about, blogs get really boring really fast.

Bloggers want to love your product. In fact, we want to love your product as much as or more than you do. There's nothing we like better than becoming fans of a new and outstanding app or accessory.

Finding that new hotness is the addictive pursuit of those of us who write for online tech sites. Each day, we sift through mounds of the boring, ordinary, and just plain bad.

When we discover something that sparkles and makes our pulse race, we reach for our keyboards. It's a real high to be the first kid on the block to play with something that's innovative, different, and excellent.

More than that, however, we have an urge to share our excitement. We're technology's natural evangelists and gossips. Forget about hidden gems; we want to post to our daily audiences of hundreds of thousands of regular readers and tell them about the new goodies we've just found.

To be a blog reviewer is to endlessly explore the mediocre in hopes of finding those few outstanding items. The app that uplifts us, the accessory that helps us use our systems in new ways, the game that becomes addictive, the utility that we can't do without… these are the treasures that we're endlessly on the hunt for.

Unfortunately, we cannot uncover those great finds without your help. We are overwhelmed by the daily minutia of countless review submissions. Unless you take the time to lead us to your product, to take us by the hand, to talk to us in small easily understood phrases, we're probably going to miss the greatness of what you have on offer.

When dealing with bloggers, you must accept a few basic facts:

- We are overwhelmed.
- At best, we have the attention span of a 3-year-old.
- We are always under deadline for some other write-up that takes priority over yours.

In other words, as a key audience for promoting your product, bend over backwards to get us to understand what you're saying and make us pay attention to you. Communicate the value of your product quickly, effectively, and succinctly.

Enter this book. *Pitch Perfect* is all about how to communicate with bloggers. It takes you through the process of review, discussing how your product enters the flow, what happens along the way, and how you can best ensure that you create the best possible relationship with your reviewer.

Think of this book as a blogger "care and feeding" guide. It reveals the ins and outs of the real world that lies behind the home pages of websites and helps you navigate common pitfalls.

How This Book Is Organized

Pitch Perfect uncovers the veil behind blogs and shows you what really happens on the road to your product's review. Here's a rundown of what you find in this book:

- **How Blogs Work**—This chapter introduces the daily basics of real-world blogs. You learn where your pitch ends up at the other end of the email chain and what happens to it from there, as reviewers evaluate whether they want to bite or not.

- **The Attractive Product**—A review is a subjective thing and yet certain universal truths apply, regardless of who does the evaluation. Discover what qualities reviewers are looking for, and learn how to integrate these into your development plans from the very start, not just when you're ready to go to market.

- **Crafting Your Pitch**—Clear communication is the heart of your pitching story. Even the best products can be overlooked when you fail to express yourself succinctly and comprehensibly. Learn what elements go into a good pitch and how to put them together to create effective communication.

- **Pitching Do's and Don'ts**—As bloggers, we see people make the same mistakes over and over. This section shows you how to bypass common pitfalls that can endanger your marketing success.

- **Case Studies**—Good pitches excite, intrigue, and engage. Bad pitches, at best, amuse. The examples in this chapter highlight both successful pitches and the ones that need improvement. You see what works in each of these pitches and what needs a bit of attention as we share real-world examples of pitches from our inbox.

- **Preparing for PR**—From websites to videos, pitches are more than just a simple email. In this chapter, you read about the supporting material that helps you market better and more successfully.

- **The Care and Feeding of Your Blogger**—Not every review is a good one, and not every reviewer loves what you have to offer. Here are some simple strategies that you can use to respond to both good and negative coverage and build a working relationship with bloggers.

- **Worksheets and Checklists**—Make sure that your product is ready for marketing using these handy worksheets.

In this book, we provide our accumulated knowledge about how to develop effective pitches. As long-time tech bloggers, we've seen our share of short and sweet pitches that capture our attention and shared a good laugh at some dismal failures.

We'll share tips on how to help your pitch avoid inbox deletion, describe ways to keep tech bloggers in the loop about what you're working on, and point you in the right direction on maintaining good relations with the public and the press.

Ready to get started? Read on to learn the ins and outs of a successful website pitch.

How Blogs Work

Thinking about marketing your product? Prepare for a whirlwind. You're about to enter an ADHD world that's limited on attention span and desperate for new and exciting hotness. You've got to be sharp, focused, and exactly on point, because your opportunity to present yourself is even more fleeting than you might imagine.

Each and every blogger alive is tragically short on time. Bloggers always have too much mail to get through and too little time to give each product the attention it deserves. This is the core truth about our work lives. You'll need to catch a blogger's interest in just a few seconds.

That tiny interval of time when you pass across that blogger's radar is critical. It's the one chance you have to make that first impression and sell yourself and your product. Are you ready for that moment? For that second?

We bloggers are dying to find the product that we're going to absolutely love. A blogger's golden chalice is represented, for example, by an app that stays on our phone and is used constantly, or by the must-have accessory that makes our lives easier and more fun. It's the t-shirt that everyone wants to buy or the Etsy item that redefines a whole market space.

Bloggers love to discover and then gush about that discovery. That passion is what blogging is all about.

A Typical Day at a Major Blog

We work at a major tech blog, part of AOL's network. Every month, we deal with millions of readers, with all the joys and headaches that involves. Being a blogger is an amazing experience. It allows you to network with all kinds of readers on a scale that personal blogging can't. We connect, we analyze, we offer opinions, we create reviews. It's a privilege for all of us and an unparalleled opportunity, but it's one that demands a lot from the blogger. Blogging is not a low-stress occupation.

Our typical day at The Unofficial Apple Weblog (http://www.tuaw.com/tag/tuawtvlive) (see Figure 1-1) begins like this. We grab breakfast, arm ourselves with steaming hot cups of coffee or cans of Mountain Dew, and sit down to sort through the press releases that arrived during the night. That sounds like a pretty easy way to start the day, right?

Wrong. At TUAW and most of the other large tech blogs, we're inundated every day of the week with a flood of press releases. It's not just a dozen or so; in a typical weekday, we look at well over a hundred PR blasts, all of which are trying to get us excited about a specific app or accessory. But, that's just the start.

Figure 1-1
Steve and Erica blog at The Unofficial Apple Weblog, www.tuaw.com.

Review Requests

Press releases arrive from a variety of sources, including individual companies and distribution services, like PRMac (http://prmac.com/) and PRWeb (http://www.prweb.com/). Many developers work on a shoestring. They don't have the money to spend on these press release services, which distribute to hundreds of news outlets.

Instead, most Apple developers pick a target group of blogs (usually those like TUAW with a huge readership) and email them a direct pitch. Besides TUAW, popular Apple review sites include macworld.com, macrumors.com, arstechnica.com, 9to5mac.com, engadget.com, theverge.com, imore.com, mactech.com, macobserver.com, ilounge.com, macstories.com, appleinsider.com, and cultofmac.com, among many others.

But, pitching isn't limited to just our world. Product developers should build their own roster of interest-related blogs. For example, many Etsy sellers and deviantArt artists work with sites like io9.com, neatorama.com, themarysue.com, blastr.com, geeksofdoom.com, and laughingsquid.com. Political writers might focus on getting their books mentioned on salon.com, dailykos.com, instapundit.com, and so forth.

Email pitches transform our morning flood into a roaring torrent of breathless descriptions of new, unique, and absolutely amazing apps and accessories. This raging stream continues throughout the workday.

Sadly, most products aren't new or unique. Press releases are often poorly written. They flicker in front of our glazed eyes for only a moment before we click the button that sends the message to trash. Add in the notices from some developers who find it necessary to send out full press releases for every miniscule version update to their apps, and it's easy to see why we're overwhelmed.

Our goal is not to depress you, but the honest truth is that out of every hundred PR blasts we see, at most, one or two products get reviewed. Most press releases get a look over and then move straight into trash. A very low percentage of these requests continue on to posts on our site.

For developers, exposure on major websites provides an essential component of business success, even if it's not the complete answer to that success. Even a glowing review on TUAW or another major website cannot guarantee your app a spot in the New & Noteworthy category on the top of the iTunes App Store or create a bestseller on Amazon.

Regardless, it always helps developers to place their product in front of a large audience. We often hear from developers who say that they received a huge bounce in sales from a single post on TUAW. We call it the *TUAWlanche* effect, and we're delighted when products we've championed find their audience and achieve success.

Smaller Blogs

How do you find minor blogs as well as the big name ones? Consider hopping into iTunes or Amazon, surveying competing products, and discovering where their pull quotes from good reviews originated.

At the same time, weigh the time and effort against returns. TUAW blogger Kelly Guimont points out, getting the word out to every small blog possible might take more time than you anticipate and, in the end, you "find out that both their readers already bought your product. You could have spent that time crafting a glorious pitch for Engadget instead."

🎙 **NOTE**

Any blog that replies to your pitch asking for a fee to "expedite review" is a scam. Avoid them.

Making Sausage: How Reviews Happen

"It's too bad that none of the apps I get pinged about are really of interest to me, and often downright sloppy. The first step to making it big in the App Store should be making a good app, methinks."

—Brett Terpstra, TUAW blogger, web and app developer

"I don't know that app developers and marketing managers are really aware of what a really good review takes out of a blogger and how even though they may be giving us a $6 app, or even a $60 keyboard, my time and energy is worth so much more than that. Even if the "work" is fun, it's still testing and putting something through its paces and it's still work. I run a small consulting business and a family. It's really hard for me to justify giving away free or really low-cost advertising for someone else. My family and my health come first, and my friends, too! This is why I've had to scale back my review posting, but I really want to get back into it, just in a healthier way."

—Melissa Davis, TheMacMommy (http://www.themacmommy.com/)

To better understand how bloggers decide what makes it to the home page and what gets thrown into the email trash, consider how bloggers actually put together their reviews and what they're looking for. It's a bit like making sausages.

The end product is a lot prettier and tastier than the process itself might indicate. Otto von Bismarck once said, "If you like laws and sausages, you should never watch either one being made." The same advice goes for doing reviews. Trying to find good review fodder among the onslaught of pitches can be a frustratingly inefficient process.

What Do Bloggers Look For?

Bloggers live for the product that is exciting, newsworthy, different, or extremely useful to write about. When a product doesn't fit one of those criteria, it's likely to be overlooked. At TUAW, we deal mostly with apps and accessories. While we focus on Apple-related software and hardware, other blogs might cover books, automobiles, fashion, photography, and other merchandise.

What we have to say about the *way* we in which we review items transfers to these other arenas. The experience of human excitement is universal. So, if you're reading this book and you create Café Press and Zazzle items or you are an author trying to get your book reviewed, adjust our criteria accordingly. These apply to other blogs, other products, and other interests.

Here's a list of what we specifically look for in apps. Certain qualities jump out and make us take notice. The kinds of apps we want to review offer these features.

An *exciting* app is either completely unique (something quite rare) or achieves its utility in an attention-grabbing way. An exciting app makes you stop, think, and react. They inspire a "wow, that's cool" reaction. There are hundreds of thousands apps in the App Store. "Me too" apps make our eyes glaze over whenever we see the press releases for them. The exciting app? That's what we live for.

We recently found an app that scanned automobile VIN numbers and instantly offered wholesale and retail pricing estimates, including Bluebook values and more. Within an hour, nearly every blogger at TUAW had downloaded that app and used it to scan their car. That kind of app is exciting, or as one of our readers put it, "Erica, Thank you for this article! This is one of the most useful apps I've ever downloaded! It is so easy to use and provides great information with little effort." That is what we look for in an exciting app.

Newsworthy apps fit into a larger story. When an app fits an ongoing narrative that's caught the attention of the blogosphere, it provides a coverage hook for bloggers. This allows us to tie app coverage concretely into current events and promote that app as part of the story. During the Hurricane Sandy floods (no relation to co-author Steve Sande), we actively looked for apps that supported offsite backup to help guard against natural disasters.

When a developer transforms a pedestrian concept to create an app that achieves its goals in a new way that is faster, better, more connected, or just plain more fun, we sit up and take notice. *Different* matters. There's no reason for developers to mimic the functionality and even the UI of every other app in its category, so why not start by creating something that's special?

If you do, and if your press release is focused on pointing out the advantages over competing apps and showcasing features that aren't available anywhere else, you're going to get our attention.

To be fair, one infamous app was designed to let users text and drive. It offered new and different functionality, and it did its job well, but we dismissed it in the end—it was suitable only for Darwin Award winners.

Function matters, too. We don't care how pretty your app is if it does something *extremely useful*. Yes, an ugly app with a bad UI that does something amazing *can* win our hearts, like Ambrosia's Snapz Pro X. It's an OS X screenshot utility with all the design aesthetics of the former Soviet Bloc. But, we reviewed it positively when it finally updated for Mountain Lion. Apps that improve our lives and help us get things done are always welcome. If your app creates some functionality we haven't seen before and does it well, that's going to catch our eye. At least it usually will.

Developer *devotion and commitment* also play important roles, especially when an app or product offers complex features and/or synchronization capabilities. In exchange for product investment by users, be prepared to step up to the plate on a regular basis with updates, bug fixes, and improvements based on user feedback.

Why Do Bloggers Review?

Blogs are an advertising-driven business. We write posts including news, reviews, and help articles to attract a large audience. We want to grow that audience so we can sell ads on the site for revenue. Without the ads and audience, we're not getting paid.

But, it's not just about business. Bloggers are addicted to writing and to community. We love discovering things and telling people about them. In the case of tech bloggers, It's all about the latest thing. There's nothing we love more than getting excited about a new app or tech product and sharing that excitement with others.

We blog because we're curious, because we love trying things out, and because we love talking about the experience of trying things out. We serve an audience that wants to know whether an item is a good buy and/or a great value. The audience wants to know what new apps are worthy of a spot on their home screen or a place in their gear bags.

There's so much information, so little time. We serve those who let us do that job for them. To the reader, it's a free consultation; a chance to pick the brains of an IT professional.

🎙 **NOTE**

During a recent podcast, we were asked if we made special exceptions to review products from "superstar" celebrity developers. Our response? Hell yes! Celebrity drives page views, and page views drive our paychecks. It may not be fair, but it's a fact of life.

Attracting Readers

We attract readers by writing about new products, including apps or accessories. Readers want to know the details about a product—things like the price, availability, and features. They also want opinion. Bloggers help entice them to purchase the product or warn them to steer clear. Blogging isn't journalism. It's opinion writing flavored with passion and personal experience.

When an app is really awful, we usually pass on the opportunity to review it. Most bloggers won't go out of their way to trash a new app that doesn't make the cut.

Providing Criticism

Steve once had a developer who wrote a wonderful pitch about his educational app. The application *sounded* great, but when loaded and launched, it was one of the worst he had ever seen. It was filled with misspellings, the user interface resembled an unsolvable puzzle, and some of the text was so small (and non-resizable) that it was unreadable. To top it off, the app repeatedly crashed.

The app was essentially an amateurish attempt to repackage old CD-ROM content for mobile devices; it was awful. Rather than embarrass the developer publicly and potentially ruin any chance of him ever selling another app, Steve wrote him a personal email telling him of his concerns for the app, explaining why he wasn't going to review it.

Although Steve provided constructive criticism, the developer remained adamant on one point. He truly believed his app was really well done. It wasn't. Several horrible reviews were subsequently published by other blogs, proving that it wasn't just Steve who found the app awful. We hope that the dev decides to fix the glaring issues with his app.

Most bloggers aren't out there to make you feel like a failure. For the most part, we point out the good and not-so-good features of your product in their reviews. We want to provide valuable information to our readers, not make fun of you or other product developers. You can best help us by crafting items that we're going to be enthusiastic about reviewing. Always send in your best work.

Product developers who listen to blogger criticism and use it to improve their products are much more likely to receive the repeated attention of bloggers in the form of reviews. Developer Saied Ghaffari of It's About Time Products (http://www.helloiat.com/) creates training and other apps for Apple's iOS and Mac platforms. Steve made a comment in one post several years ago noting that the name of one app—"It's About Time: Learn the Switch to Mac"—was a mouthful and difficult to fit into a blog headline.

Recently, Saied pitched a new ebook and app, and both had succinct names: "Hello Mac OS X" and "Hello iPhoto." He pointed out in a conversation with Steve that he had listened to the feedback and took it to heart. Did it make Steve feel good that a developer had responded to criticism in a positive way? Sure! Did that positive response color Steve's decision to review Saied's new products on TUAW? Absolutely.

How Do Bloggers Perform Evaluations?

When a blogger evaluates a new or revised product, it's generally because we saw something that really caught our eye. Something "popped." It grabbed our attention and made us take notice. At that point, we often ask for a review unit or, in the case of apps, a promo code, but we do so with no guarantees or promises attached.

Making these requests doesn't always mean that we'll write about it. Remember that subpar app Steve looked at? He received a promo code, but applied that admonition we all hear from our parents: "If you can't say any-thing nice about a person, keep quiet."

That doesn't mean we don't publish negative reviews. We do. Sometimes, we do this because we have a point to make about the app or its quality. More often, we do because we have an editorial calendar that requires service. You cannot commit to an iPhone-, iPad-, or Mac-App-of-the-Day without writing up *some* app.

For the most part, bloggers prefer to skip products they don't like as well as the vast oceans of the mediocre. Doing so is not always practical, especially in a daily business where content drives readership, readership drives ad views, and ad views drive paychecks.

For many bloggers, reviews are a daily fact of life and, as much as we would prefer to highlight the special, the terrific, and the exceptional, we spend a lot of time navigating the common, the tedious, and the adequate.

Performing the Review

So, how do we evaluate? We can't speak for all bloggers, but we'll give you an idea of the process we personally use for reviews. We start with app reviews. A discussion of hardware reviews follows in the next section. If you're coming to this book with a different kind of product, make sure to read both sections because they contain hints as to how reviews take place on real-world blogs.

Our evaluation begins by looking at the description of the app on the App Store. Has the developer provided a concise description of what the app does? Does the pitch include screenshots or a video that shows off details of the user interface in action? All these items make a good—or bad—first impression on us.

We install the app. Do we run into any difficulties installing the app? Apps should load quickly, launch perfectly the first time, and provide a fast and simple setup. We note when the app crashes the first time launched, or if we can't get the app configured in a few minutes.

Next, we use the app in the manner in which it is intended. If it's a game, we'll see if it grabs our attention and holds it for more than just a few minutes. Steve was sent an "Angry Birds" clone to review that looked pretty darned good at first glance. After a few minutes of play, he found that the app would occasionally skip levels for no known reason, and he quickly reached a level that he could not win. Frustration set in, and he soon stopped using the app. It didn't get a glowing review.

We look at when the app was last updated. If it's been several months to over a year since an update was issued, we question whether the developer is devoted and committed to utilizing user feedback to make improvements or provide stability in an ever-changing operating system ecosystem. Would you enjoy eating stale bread?

When the app is complex and/or expensive (over $4.99 U.S.), we check if it offers a free or "lite" version. Many users want to take apps for test drives before making long-term commitments.

We look to see how the app fits within a developer's related offerings, not just as a standalone item. Are all the good bits of the app hidden behind in-app upgrade pay walls? Is the app covered in advertisements or cross promotion? Those are usually hints that developers are looking at users as cash cows, not valued customers.

Then, there's data entry. How well does the app safeguard your data? Entering data demands a huge investment of time; an app needs to be reliable and offer data backups, exports, and imports, perhaps via iCloud or Dropbox. Does it do that?

Basically, we look at the app holistically, as if we were the target users testing it out in the most common conditions we can manage. We run it through its paces and try to use it in as near real-life conditions as possible.

What About Accessories and Other Hardware?

We approach hardware reviews with the same steps as we do software, but we try out each product out using as many real-world conditions as possible. We bring the item into the field and use it as the developer recommended. We feel it, manipulate it, and try to give it a full workout in the ways we think it might encounter during normal use. If you say that an iPad case is completely waterproof, we're going to test that claim, even if it means that we're risking ruining our expensive hardware for a review.

We're looking to see if the hardware is well made. We check to see if it's easy to break. Most importantly, we try to decide if the item does what it promises in the marketing text. Does it fulfill the basic utility promised by the vendor?

Many items that sound like great ideas on the website when you're clicking Purchase don't work as well in real use. We pay attention to battery life, connectors, durability, and convenience. If a battery booster weighs 5 pounds, you're not likely to carry it around in your pocket with your phone.

The endpoint of hardware reviews is to provide an evaluation of whether the product is solid and offers good value.

Elements of Review

The kind of item you ship off for review can influence the style of the review that takes place. Because we work a lot with apps, let's explain that in an app context. Here are some ways we treat various app categories.

Business apps are always a challenge to review. If they're focused on a specific task and do that well, they'll receive a good review. Apps that try to do too many things usually end up doing nothing well. There's an online small-business accounting service, Kashoo (https://www.kashoo.com/), that Steve has been using for some time. The iPad app acts as a mobile frontend for this service. It's easier to use than the online service itself. In his estimation, that's worth a good review.

Photo apps tend to be one of two types: those that help you take better photos through a different frontend to the built-in cameras of new iOS devices, and those used to add effects to those flawless photos. There's one issue with the latter type: There are just too many apps that try to do the same thing. What makes one of these apps stand out? It's one with lots of effects, the ability to tweak effects, and a clear user interface.

For the frontend type of photo apps, two specific products jump out as perfect examples of what bloggers love to hear about. The first is Camera+, which is a photo taking and editing app that first gained notoriety when it was kicked out of the Apple App Store. That was newsworthy, but the continuing additions of new and unique features to the app make it something worth writing about again and again.

The second app is Occipital's 360 Panorama, which was the first panorama app to use the gyroscope and accelerometer built into recent versions of the iPhone and iPad to take seamless, automatic panoramic photos. The distinctive way that the app enables anyone to create and view beautiful panoramas by just waving an iOS device around caught our attention in the crowded field of photography apps.

Another big area for apps is *social networking*. There are way too many Twitter apps on the App Store in our opinion, especially since recent iOS and OS X releases embrace Twitter and add support for the official app. Yet, there is still a place for Twitter apps that add features that aren't found in the eponymous app. If you can differentiate your app with a new twist on Twitter API feature, you can grab a good review.

Tweetbot from Tapbots LLC is an ideal case of a Twitter app that goes well beyond the built-in functionality and adds features that make the app well worth more than the $2.99 purchase price. We eagerly anticipate news of updates to this app, and it's never failed to surprise and delight our blogging team.

We could go on through all the different app genres, but we hope you get the general idea by now: quality and uniqueness matter. That applies no matter what product you're developing and what blog you're submitting to. Instead, here's a summary of some of the things we focus on as we perform a review.

Graphics and Design

When a product provides adequate functionality, beautiful design and colorful graphics can give it a slight edge in a review. Be sure to make your app look good and make text readable and clear. The same qualities apply to hardware. A well-designed unit, with intrinsically beautiful and well-made features, makes us sit up and take notice.

Even a distinctive app icon can make the difference in whether or not your app attracts the attention of a blogger. Several of the TUAW bloggers chose the Tweetbot icon (see Figure 1-2) as a favorite, because it's eye-catching and represents the robot theme inherent in the Tapbots line of apps.

Figure 1-2
Tweetbot's icon is eye-catching, smart, relevant, and memorable.

Here's another idea: Use a color other than blue for your app icon. A vast majority of app icons seem to use the same blue background, which makes it difficult for users and bloggers to discern a difference between apps. An icon that is colorful and describes at a glance what your app does can go a surprisingly long way toward snagging a review.

User Interface

An app or device that presents a clean and intuitive user interface wins, in our opinion. It doesn't matter what the product is designed to do; if the UI makes sense, follows standard UI guidelines, and we can figure out what to do with it in seconds, it's going to get our attention.

Take the Clear app, for example (see Figure 1-3). It's a to-do list manager with a superior and colorful multitouch UI, and it has gained lots of fans. That kind of interface differentiation can, and will, catch our eye.

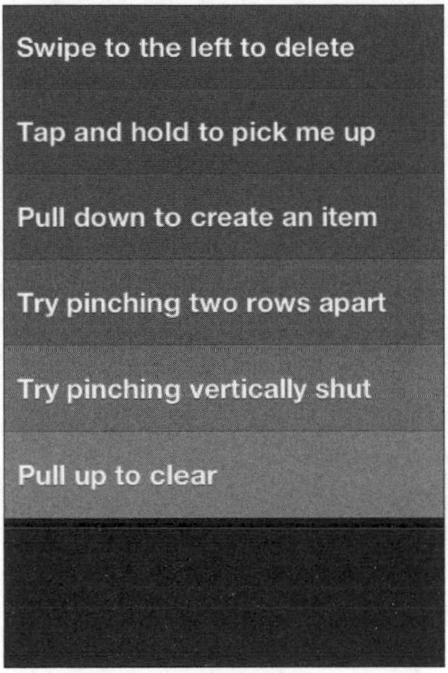

Swipe to the left to delete

Tap and hold to pick me up

Pull down to create an item

Try pinching two rows apart

Try pinching vertically shut

Pull up to clear

Figure 1-3
Clear offers a terrific example of excellent GUI design.

Visual design extends beyond apps, of course. It's one of the key components for any product on the marketplace. A brilliantly designed poster will sell, as will a well-crafted kitchen gadget. Good design always engages a reviewer.

Value

Does a product provide exceptional value for the money? Steve purchased and used a PDF markup app for his iPad that cost $9.99. One day, Erica told him about another app that was free during the introductory period, had a beautiful and easy-to-understand UI, and had more useful features. If you think we were excited about this app, you're right.

Value doesn't mean cheap. The Mac's dictionary offers this definition, which is perfect: "the worth of something compared to the price paid or asked for it." The PDF markup app won't always be free. But, even at a price equal to its competitors, it would provide more value as it has more utility and an outstanding user interface.

If your product offers excellent value, it will find its audience and appeal to a reviewer.

Utility

The dictionary describes utility as a noun, meaning, "the state of being useful, profitable, or beneficial." When discussing the utility of a product, we like to compare it to the adjective "useful, especially through being able to perform several functions."

Food Network TV host Alton Brown often derides certain kitchen utensils for being "uni-taskers" that take up space and have only one use. He loves kitchen gadgets that can be used for a variety of purposes. We feel the same way about products that let us do several things and get rid of other products.

That's not to say that a product that performs a single task very well won't fit the bill when it comes to utility. If it is very useful and does the job it is designed for with flair and finesse, we usually give it a good write-up. Any additional tasks it can perform are often icing on the cake and functions that raise a good product to excellence.

Settings

Settings are, admittedly, a software-specific quality, although other products can suffer from an excess of user-tweakable features. Nothing irritates reviewers more than apps with too many settings and no explanation of the benefit of each one. If an app takes too long to set up before it's useful, we'll usually quickly remove it from our devices. Apps that have well thought-out settings that can be made or changed in a few moments make us happy.

Apps that lead a user through a quick setup and tour process on the first launch receive a thumbs-up from Steve. If an app is set up properly in the first few seconds of use and the developer then points out functions of interest, the app is more likely to be explored by the user than become a confusing nuisance that takes up home screen real estate.

One other thought about settings: Think about where you put them. Many new and experienced iOS users completely forget to look at the Settings app (see Figure 1-4) when they're using an app. Place as many of your settings into the body of the app as you can, and avoid hiding them in the Settings app. These days, most developers limit their Settings entries to legal notices.

Figure 1-4
Although Apple provides a centralized Settings app, many users are unaware of its existence and how it is used to adjust settings for a number of apps.

Options

Another criterion that bloggers consider while reviewing is whether options (upgrades for apps, accessories for hardware) are available. Developers can provide a "base" app that performs a certain task well, and then make optional features available to customers through "pro" versions of the app or in-app purchases.

We're okay with being able to try out an app at a minimal cost, then adding functionality by going "pro." This pricing structure is often known as the "freemium" model, with developers giving away the base app, and then charging for additional or premium features.

In any case, the base app or base product has to stand on its own. Nothing irritates us more than a product that spends its time trying to sell more stuff. If your product looks more like an ad than a solution, you've lost our attention.

Features

Looking at the dictionary again, features are defined as "distinctive aspects or attributes of something." In terms of reviews, features are those items that set apart a product as uniquely different from its competitors.

A feature can be a capability that nobody has achieved before, a beautiful and unique design, or a different way to perform a function. Products with features that are useful, functional, and well-designed make reviewers take notice.

Erica recently reviewed a series of smart dongles that integrated with the iPhone (the Wallet TrackR). She loved that, in addition to being able to find your keys on demand by sounding an audible alert, the unit would remind you if you walked too far away from them. This passive "you forgot your keys" feature made a huge difference in the way she appreciated and reviewed the product, and it excited readers who plan to use the device to make sure they don't leave their overcoats behind at restaurants.

Finish

Too many products are rushed to market before they're fully finished, debugged, tested, refined, and polished. If you feel a push to just "put something out there," rethink your strategy. A rushed product is a bad-review magnet. Your later updates and sales may never recover from an initially flawed launch.

If you find yourself sending letters like the following on a regular basis, you're missing the point about adding product finish:

Thanks for taking the time to review [app]. We learned a great deal from your critique and integrated many of your suggestions into the application, resulting in a product that provides a more efficient "Getting Things Done" analysis.

[A long list of features that have been changed]

My hope is that you will update your review after giving [app] another try. As a thank you, I'd like to offer a link to share with your visitors that will allow the first 30 visitors to download free versions of [app]: [url].

Sadly, most blogs rarely revisit a review, no matter how kindly you ask us to. If we think your product has promise, we may offer early criticism via a phone call or email and invite you to resubmit once the product is more likely to receive a better review. Take this offer seriously.

I also think that it's very important that developers make sure that your app is completely polished and ready for release, before actually releasing it. Too many times, I see developers release an app that they are 80% happy with, as they see the potential down the line with updates. Unfortunately, reviewers are only going to look at the current incarnation, not the potential.

—Brian Akaka of Appular, on TUAW Marketing Chat 2010 (http://www.tuaw. com/2010/01/15/tuaw-livechat-promoting-your-app-store-products/)

Steve, as the hardware editor at TUAW, sees another finish problem on a regular basis: the hardware prototype. In this situation, manufacturers eager for a review send a prototype of a product to a blogger.

Although the products are usually close to their final form, there can be the occasional quirk with a prototype that needs to be worked out. Even worse is the case where we ask the manufacturer when the product will become available, and they basically have no money to do a production run; they're hoping that the publicity they gain from a great review will entice their backers to reach into their wallets for more funding.

Trust us; we'd rather write about a product that is in production. If you're having issues with getting enough funding to produce a product in sellable quantities, perhaps you need to rethink your plans, find a new backer, or consider crowd-sourced funding through Kickstarter (more about that later).

How Much Time Is Spent Reviewing Each Product?

Quality matters. The better a product is, the higher the probability is that a reviewer will really "look under the hood" and search out each and every feature in it. A product that excites reviewers receives lots of hands-on love. A poorly developed one that breaks down, crashes constantly, or has an unusable user interface gets quickly tossed.

Consider apps. Unique concepts, fun games, or social-networking apps that engage the reviewer (and by default, anyone who installs the app) are often apps that we use religiously in the future. One recent example was a unique health app/service called The Eatery. Steve decided to give it a spin.

This app and service obtains crowd-sourced opinions of how healthy you are eating. Steve decided not use the app permanently, but thought that it would be interesting during the testing to have a number of opinions on how healthy his eating habits were. He decided to keep the app on his iPhone 4S and use it for a few weeks.

This long-term use gave him a really good feel for the app, the service, and how the crowd-sourced food scores worked. Had he just based a review on the look and feel of the app, it would have received a good review. The experience of working with the app over a period of time gave insight into things he liked and hated about it. His total time spent using the app? Probably two hours in total.

That's one end of the spectrum. On the other end are special-use products that are created for a small niche market. While we try to match bloggers to the product, sometimes a blogger will find that she or he is not familiar with the use that the item is designed for. What happens with those? Usually, they just get a cursory review of features and design, without the detail that a really in-depth review requires. In a case like this, your product may be given only 15 minutes of attention. And that's a shame if it's really worthy of more love.

What Kind of Timeline Crunch Are Reviewers Under?

At TUAW and many of the other large blogs, we have an editorial calendar for reviews (see Figure 1-5). That means that we get information about products, but we have several days or weeks to use it prior to writing a review. On the other hand, if a product is considered to be "hot" and is getting a lot of attention from our competitors, we try to get a review out as soon as possible, often on the day of release.

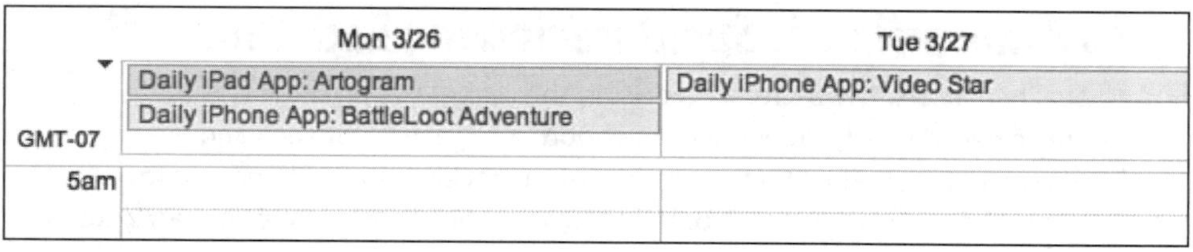

	Mon 3/26	Tue 3/27
	Daily iPad App: Artogram	Daily iPhone App: Video Star
GMT-07	Daily iPhone App: BattleLoot Adventure	
5am		

Figure 1-5
Many sites now use a review schedule.

Do we rush reviews? No. Our goal is to provide a fair-and-balanced review for our readers, so we'll try every feature, try to resolve any issues ourselves, and talk with the developers if something really odd is happening. We give just about every product the attention it deserves. Remember, we want to provide our readers with a service that they'll keep coming back for. If they find that they're reading a poorly researched and hastily written review, they won't be back.

How Long Does It Take to Tell You're Trying Out a Lemon?

After looking at probably several thousand apps and a huge number of accessories, we can tell pretty quickly if an app or accessory is a "keeper" or if it's heading toward uninstall or the hardware giveaway pile (see Figure 1-6). Many times, that first impression takes less than a minute. If the product shows even a bit of promise, we'll go further and try out more of the feature set. Apps that are junk get deleted immediately.

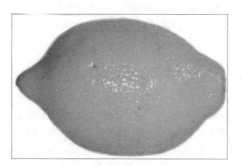

Figure 1-6
A lemon (*Citrus limon*) quickly calls attention to itself during initial review.

The product tells us its story. If it crashes or cannot be used from the get-go, that story ends quickly. If it engages us and invites us to continue using it, our testing can go on for hours. With hardware, that testing can even go days or weeks.

The very best products are the ones we jump into our chat room and tell each other about. "You've got to try this" means we've got a live one on the hook. For those kinds of products, your review may receive input from several bloggers, all of them testing it out, often on our own dime.

If you can get bloggers to go out and buy your product just so they can contribute to a review write-up, you have a winner on your hands.

What Kinds Of Reviews Do Bloggers Write?

Bloggers don't usually write just one type of review. There are several ways that we can approach information about products that are pitched to us. We use these different styles to create a variety of write-ups on our site. Depending on your product and what we consider to be its newsworthiness, it may receive one or more of these posts.

First Look

The simplest write-up is what we call a *first look*. A first-look review is gener-ally written when we get an app or accessory that is "hot" and we want to give readers some information about it as soon as possible. This type of review cov-ers the bare essentials that a reader needs to know: what the product does, how much it costs, any special features (like accessories or in-app purchase, different levels for a game, etc.), what it compares to, and what the developer is well-known for (if he's written a number of apps or shipped other hardware). First-look reviews often get a follow-up in-depth review, especially if we want to keep up with the news cycle before we have a chance to sit down and look at the product in more detail.

Overview

The next level of depth is an *overview*. This may be a product that isn't get-ting a lot of press, but is something that we're interested in. Overview reviews give a reader an idea of what the product does, what the cost is, and how it compares feature-wise with other apps or hardware, but then goes into more depth of what the product actually does and how it works.

Hands On

The *hands-on* review is usually written after a blogger has had a chance to work with a product for a while. In this type of review, a blogger often talks about using the product to address a particular use case. It may not necessar-ily go into a lot of detail about competing products, but it's a good way for readers to get an idea of exactly what an app or hardware can or cannot do. We often contact the developer during a hands-on review so we can better understand the product as we test it.

In Depth

The *in-depth* review is where the reviewer describes every last little detail of the product, discusses the developer's experience and compares it with simi-lar products, takes a huge number of photos or screenshots to demonstrate unique or different features of the product or user interface, and even offers suggestions on how the product can be improved. In-depth reviews take the most time, which is why they're also the least likely type of review you'll receive.

Choosing a Review Type

How do bloggers determine what kind of review to write? In many cases, it's based on previous history with the developer, the price of the product, and just how newsworthy the blogger feels that the product is. As an example, bloggers at TUAW have reviewed many different apps for reading and anno-tating PDF files, so most incoming PDF annotation apps get a cursory review or are just pulled into a roundup of new items. However, when one appeared that did the job faster, better, and cheaper (and for free), we jumped on it with a hands-on review.

A product that's more expensive or sophisticated in functionality is probably going to receive an in-depth review, simply because the blogger needs to put a lot of time and effort into digging into the details.

Why Blog Reviews Matter

Blog reviews mean exposure. Big blogs mean bigger exposure. It's as simple as that. Want to develop a big audience? The bigger the blog exposure, the more you benefit, especially if your product is solid and receives a good review.

How big? Here's a real-world reaction from Dave Clarke of Kashoo, telling us how a TUAW review influenced his sales:

Wanted to relay some numbers to you. In terms of iPad app downloads, the TUAW review led to our biggest day ever at 7x the average day at that time and 1.5x the previous biggest day. We had more downloads of the app in the 3 days after the review than the previous 2 weeks combined. The immediate effect was a substantial 4-day lift (almost 300% over previous 3 days; and, over previous Monday-Thursday).

BigBlueCouch received a nice boost from our in:play write-up. Here's what its creative director had to say in a follow-up email to us:

I and the rest of the team at BigBlueCouch want to give you a big thank you for your review of in:play on TUAW! We can't thank you enough. Your article kicked off a landslide and in one day we went from being non-existent in the app store to #64 overall in the United States, #4 in Music, and made it into the New and Noteworthy category. Thank you!!! Just wanted to give you an update and express our deep appreciation.

These reactions are typical. A big positive push can launch your product to a larger audience. One small developer sent us a trends chart showing a 6,400% boost in sales for a game app that was otherwise orphaned in App Store obscurity.

Victor Agreda, our editor-in-chief, has stated that TUAW frequently drives more sales and downloads of an app than an Apple feature in the App Store. TUAW and other blogs act as readers' "trusted friends." A blog site's opinions are very influential compared to banners, which customers treat as simple "billboard on the highway."

The chart in Figure 1-7 comes from developer Lyle Andrews. We featured Lyle's app Fireworks HD as our Mac App of the Day on December 27, 2011. Its "Top Paid Entertainment" rank jumped from around #100 up to a peak of #4, and stayed in the top 10 for a while.

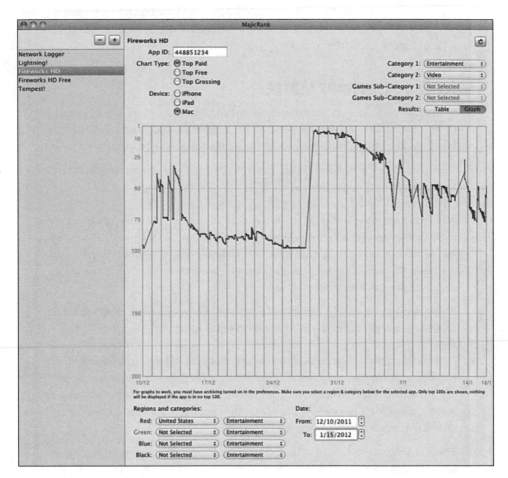

Figure 1-7
Fireworks HD market position over time.

On New Year's Eve 2012, Fireworks HD entered the "Top 10 Entertainment" charts of 13 countries. Andrews writes, "Over the next few weeks, Fireworks HD trended down as expected but happily ended in a higher average range which has persisted to date."

In other words, blog coverage *works*. It exposes your product in an unparalleled way to an audience that is specifically interested in buying these kinds of goods. The downside of this is that we're often under siege by eager devs who see us as their only hope for making their business work.

Marketing is the art of moving a product into the public eye, helping it become desirable for purchase (see Figure 1-8). Good products need word of mouth to establish an audience. Positive blog reviews help get that ball rolling and should form an important part of your marketing plan.

Figure 1-8
Blog write-ups help move products into the public eye.

At the same time, keep the following lesson in mind: It is *hard* to be an honest developer and make a go out of it, but it's not impossible. If your product is clever and noteworthy and eye- and ear-catching, it will find itself an audience. It's not easy, but good products, exciting products, always find their audience.

Marketing Realities

"Subject: promote game in appstore.

Hi, I have made very cute and interesting game for iphone. But I know that 90% of work is promotion and now I afraid to realise it. I need your advice.Thanks!!!"

—Real-world pitch request

In April 2012, marketing firm App Promo conducted a developer survey to assess success in the App Store. It found that 59% of respondents reported that they had not earned enough revenue from their most successful app to break even with development costs. What's more, 80% said that the generated revenue was not enough to sustain a standalone business.

App Promo is, of course, in the business of selling marketing services. It boasts that those developers who earned at least $50,000 from a popular app (about 12% of respondents) spent 14% of their time doing marketing, and set aside $30,000 just for their marketing budget. Less successful businesses (52% of respondents) spent 5% or less of their time on marketing and had no marketing budget at all.

There's no question that a large marketing budget helps promote an app, but for smaller indie devs, it's more often a question of what you can do with a limited budget. Blog reviews play an important role, as do press releases (a general PR blast can cost as little $25, which is pretty cheap, as these things go up to $200–$400 for a well-defined audience; see our comments later in this book about how effective [or not] press releases may be) and small, targeted ad campaigns through Google/AdMob or email blasts. You can establish a social presence on Facebook and Twitter for the cost of your time and sweat. You can participate in one of those app giveaway sites to raise your app's exposure or use a sale to try to establish a user base to give your product buzz and momentum.

If you have the capital to hire marketing help, there's a lot that paid services can do for you. If not, you need to be persistent, clever, and dedicated to get the word out for your product. As bloggers, we can play a key role in that drive for attention, but we're not the beginning and the end of your marketing tasks.

Wrapping Up

In this chapter, you discovered how blogs work and what they can do for you. Hopefully, this information helps you decide how to fit a promotion campaign targeted at blogs and reviews into your larger marketing planning.

Here are a few final thoughts to wrap up this chapter:

- Understand what blogs need (page views) and are looking for (exciting stories) and balance this with your need for publicity. Find the exciting story that already lives within your product—and emphasize that story.

- Each kind of review may offer mixed blessings. For example, with an in-depth review, you get a lot more words written about your product. On the other hand, reviewers have a lot more time to find product flaws. Target your pitch for the style of review that best showcases your product.

- Public exposure is important for any successful app. Spend time strategizing your marketing push, not just in developing the product.

2

The Attractive Product

Long, long, long before you start thinking about blogs or planning your marketing, you should be asking yourself fundamental questions. Who is the audience for my product? What niche does it fill? How does my product do its job better than any other offering currently on the market? What qualities make my product pop from the competition?

If you cannot answer these questions and, more importantly, articulate those answers in a way that excites people, you probably shouldn't be developing the product in the first place. These are strong words, are they not? But, they carry great truth: A product without intrinsic cohesive value isn't worth creating.

Any days of "if you build it, they will come" are over—if they ever existed, which we honestly doubt. Unless you have a good idea of whom you're building the product for and why people should buy it, you are essentially throwing away effort. Developing a product because it sounds like a good thing to do or because you like the *idea* of building it means you may create something that is fundamentally unsellable.

You owe yourself and your product a strong business plan that involves market differentiation and customer definition. You should fully understand how your product fits the needs of your future customer base and how it demands their attention. Strategizing is a crucial step in creating a good product. It doesn't matter if you're a large corporation or a one-man indie shop. Unless you're building *pro bono* (i.e., without interest in making money or finding an audience for your product), you need to balance your own desire for creating a sustainable business with a market demand that powers the exchange of cash or attention for goods.

Product Definition

Although pitching your product to bloggers is one of the *last* steps of product development, defining your pitch should be one of the *first*. Knowing what your product is, who it's for, and how it stands out from the competition should guide you from inception. That pitch explains why you're creating your product and why it will sell.

By the time you're ready to pitch, you should long-since know answers to the following questions. These questions define your product and help you understand why you are developing it.

The answers to these questions aren't just for pitching. They should guide the path of your development. If you're not asking these questions early (and often) in your design and building process, you're missing the best opportunity for refining and perfecting a product in advance of its marketing push.

Who Is Your Customer?

Without customers, you're not in business. You're just having a go at a hobby. You can't build a product just because you think it's cool and expect it to sell. Some do, of course, especially if they are wicked cool, but the vast majority of these attempts don't sell well at all. Chances are, your project doesn't fall into that wicked cool category that defines its own audience, and that's why you need to know to whom you're selling.

What's a wicked cool product? A perfect, recent example is the Letterpress app by star developer Loren Brichter. Because Brichter has a great deal of credibility as a developer and designer, and he had previously worked at Apple during the development of the iPhone, many people were anticipating this mystery product from him. The app, which ended up being a freemium-model two-person word game, is actually an experiment by Brichter in using a self-designed UI framework. It's not only fun to play and visually exciting, but it's also a way for Brichter to gather data on how people interact with their devices.

Part of your product development is a form of applied empathy. Visualize your customer. Try to understand how you are serving his or her needs and why that customer will want to pay you to do so. The customer doesn't yet imagine this product is in her future, so it falls to you to do that imagining.

Customers shape your product. It's pointless to build a graphing calculator for toddlers or Swarovski-studded coupon wallet for Freegans (people who eat food that has been discarded). It's critical to understand your target users and acknowledge that those users are not always just like you. Their needs are not necessarily your needs. Profile your expected consumer base and try describing your typical users.

Ask yourself why these customers need your product and why they will desire it. Always question whether the product is a proper fit. You shouldn't be trying to sell Android apps to iPhone users or expect that an app that monitors laptop battery usage will appeal to desktop users.

Do some basic math. How many potential customers fit your customer profile? What percentage of them could you appeal to? Develop the mental model of who is most likely to purchase your product and explain what this solution means for them.

What Problem Does It Solve?

Products have to do something, whether it's satisfying a need or providing an uplifting experience. Understanding what your product does and how it solves some sort of problem provides another key component in your product definition.

For games, that problem may be as simple as offering engaging entertainment. For battery boosters, it may focus on being away from the office for long periods of time. For accounting software, maybe it targets the needs of smaller shops. For medical uses, it might provide better HIPAA compliance. The answer to this question motivates your product, letting you explain in a sentence or two, the *why* of your product's existence.

For Loren Brichter, there were two markets for Letterpress: iOS device users and Brichter himself. He created an app to provide hours of entertainment to the first market and to test his UI framework for the second market.

If there's no need, there's no product. There's nothing that turns off a blogger's attention more quickly than a product that seems to be a solution to a non-existent problem. Know your need, define that need, and use that definition to explain your product's story.

How Does It Pop?

Every product should offer some kind of specific appeal that helps it stand out from the competition. It's vanishingly rare to find trailblazing products without competition in any market or arena. Ideas are cheap and development work is hard. Prepare to jump into a competitive market by expressing how your product differs from the offerings already out there.

A competitive analysis focuses on the features that make your product stand out from the crowd. It lets customers (and reviewers) understand why you can perform a task better than anyone else. Identify the features that differentiate your product and explain how those features distinguish you from the field.

As we discuss later in this book in a short section about Kickstarter, perhaps a good way to determine whether or not a product should deserve further development is to let the court of public opinion have its say. Never discount basic market research.

What Makes a Good Product?

That's a really good question, and one we ask ourselves a lot. For hardware, the product has to be useful and well made. For applications, the answer is a little more nuanced. TUAW bloggers have seen apps that are spectacularly good that never gain traction in the App Store, and mediocre apps that spend weeks in the top 10. That being said, some common themes run through good products, hardware or software.

They Have Awesome and Easily Understood User Interfaces

Consider the top apps of the last couple of years. Angry Birds has stayed on top of the bestseller list for a long time, partially because anyone can pick it up and immediately "get" how to use the slingshot to fire birds at pigs and structures.

Apple's Cards app is one of the best apps the company has developed for iOS. It's easy to use and understand, and it provides anyone with an iOS device a way to create beautiful and unique letterpress greeting cards. Many other apps also excel in this area, but we think you catch our drift here; these are apps that people use a lot because no deep thought is required to understand how they work. They're self-explanatory and don't require instructions of any type.

One common theme among bloggers is that they've tried a lot of apps and no longer have patience with non-intuitive user interfaces. Up-front user testing well in advance of your first release helps you find out early on in your development cycle whether or not your UI design makes sense.

The same criteria apply to hardware products. With hardware, interfaces mean buttons and knobs, but a simple and elegant interface is no less appreciated. Contrast Apple's original iPod minimal design with the complex music players that it was competing against. The iPod dominated the market because its touch-wheel interface was easy enough for a child to use.

App-enabled hardware—devices such as blood-pressure meters, scales, and sensors that use an app for input and to capture or analyze readings—brings an entirely new level of potential complexity to the table. Not only do developers need to know how to create a user interface that makes it easy for the hardware to do its job at the user's bidding, but they also have to be able to "hide" the complex interactions between the device and the hardware.

They Empower Users to Do Something

Whether you are developing hardware or software solutions, your product should allow users to accomplish something meaningful. Developers Nick Watt and Christiane Velen prepared a presentation a while ago that suggested that good apps "play to the strengths of mobile." That is, they make good use of communications and location-awareness and are designed for spontaneous, focused activity for short periods of use.

As an example, Watt and Velen looked at the Shazam music discovery app (see Figure 2-1). They noted how it is *spontaneous* in that you launch the app when you hear a song that you want to know the name of. You're *focused* on tasks around that song, such as telling friends about it via social networking or buying the song on iTunes.

Figure 2-1
Shazam's app simplifies music discovery for users.

It makes great use of the communications capabilities of the iPhone by accessing a remote database to tell you what song is playing, providing you with song lyrics for a spontaneous singalong, sharing the song through social media or messaging, and allowing instant purchases. Once you're done with the app, you move on to something else. This fast, short burst of usage is common with many popular apps.

They Change to Meet a User's Needs

Successful products add value for the user over time. In the case of apps, they might add new features or provide a superior set of base features that keep the user enthralled with the app. Angry Birds is a perfect example of this.

The first time most users progress through the game, they're just interested in making it to the next level. The next time around, they minimize the number of birds used to level up, with the goal of getting three stars on each level. Rovio keeps adding new levels and new versions of the app to keep players coming back for more.

Many app developers do a good job of seeking feedback from users of their apps and incorporating new features based on that feedback. Steve notes that he has used the Runkeeper app for a couple of years now to track fitness walks, and the app has evolved over that time. The UI is streamlined and there's more audible feedback, both things that make the app even easier to use and more useful to him. The app has also grown from working only with Runkeeper's own website to a solution that is integrated with over 100 partners who use the fitness data captured by Runkeeper.

Erica owns a portable mobile hotspot she uses and loves. Over time, she's discovered new ways to use the product with various devices that she never imagined at the time she purchased it. From powering her kids' Nintendo DS networks while in the car to transforming her Kindle Fire reader for Internet access, her hotspot has grown in utility. It's moved well beyond the laptop aid she originally bought it for.

Successful Developers Know Their Markets

Knowing your market means understanding what motivates buyers to choose your product over competing ones. It means keeping in constant touch with the pulse of the users (through a blog or social networking). You judge their complaints and desires, and evolve the product with features that won't detract from its focus.

One of the best examples of a development firm that uses social networking to inform potential and existing customers, as well as get feature requests and information about bugs from those customers is Tapbots, LLC (@tapbots). The company's use of Twitter and App.net is essential in its marketing of the highly successful Tweetbot and Netbot apps, as well as providing a conduit for constant customer feedback.

Even though both Steve and Erica have mixed feelings about Comcast as a service provider, its social-media strategy has been superb. Its "Comcast Bill" (http://twitter.com/comcastbill) account responds warmly and confidently to user complaints to create goodwill through outreach.

They Are Polished

Successful products are fully developed before they go to market, with a complete set of features that reflect a thorough testing process. Great developers don't ship beta. They ship solid, usable, finished products.

Too many developers misunderstand the classic quote that "real developers ship." They focus so much on getting a product out the door that they forget that the product has to be worth going out that door.

Don't create a reputation for producing half-baked, poorly executed items. Quality control matters, and it matters a lot. You already know to never ship a flawed version of your product. We implore you not to ship a sloppy version.

A few weeks of refinement can make a huge difference in the shelf life of your product—hardware or software. Take the time you need to bring your product up to the best standards you possibly can. It's worth the investment of effort.

They Keep Current

We've seen initially successful products fade into obscurity when developers failed to fix minor issues, ignored user feedback, or overwhelmed it with new bells and whistles that made it virtually unusable. Although this is worst in the software world, it applies to hardware as well, especially when proactive firmware updates could keep products active and valuable.

Listen to customer feedback and use that feedback to direct further development. Having real, live customers offers you a view of your product that you can never get through in-house conditions. Responding to them ensures that your product grows and evolves.

Keeping a database of customer feedback and how you responded to it can be a useful tool for updating existing products, fixing bugs, or even creating new products. Freshdesk (www.freshdesk.com) is a good example of such a system that can grow with your company.

They Are Relevant

Think of the intersection between the entire market and your target audience. For example, number of iOS and Android phone users who need an app to track what a newborn baby is doing is really small. The number who would actually use an app like this consistently is even smaller; most would probably (correctly) believe that they're too busy feeding the baby and changing diapers to futz around with a phone. Good products provide solutions that are relevant to their users and keep being used over time.

Why Good Interface Design Matters

There's nothing more frustrating than receiving a test device or installing an app, and then trying to figure out what it does or how to perform some function. Some developers have done a good job of making sure that you're walked through the functionality and UI of the product the first time you use it—this is what we personally like to see. A few "hint stickers" can do a world of good on hardware items. Some developers write good built-in tutorials or help files, which are helpful, but still not as nice as the walkthroughs.

We loathe products that present Byzantine user interfaces and offer no assistance to understand them. Even worse are products that require you to be online to get access to help; we can't always guarantee that we'll use a product for the first time when in range of a network.

The best apps and hardware are those that need no explanation at all. You open the package or download the app and intuitively know what to do regardless of the product's function. Way too often, we see equipment and software that the developer understands, but makes no sense to anyone else.

Avoid bad outcomes by investing in user testing. In many cases, these testers will tell you immediately what they don't like about your product, and you'll have your first warning that you need to work to make it usable. (We have some suggestions for beta test services in the following sections.)

For example, there's a specific type of app that reviewers loathe. Some developers throw together apps on a computer, yet never fully test the app on the device for which it is designed, and especially do not test that app on a multiplicity of devices, testing it across different CPU, RAM, and display conditions. That means that interactions with the app have been tested with a mouse and not with real flesh-and-blood fingers. It makes us scream with frustration.

These apps sometimes have UI features that are too small to be useful with touch interaction, but the developer obviously felt that they were fine because he or she was able to click them with a mouse in a simulator. Trust me, reviewers can tell when you have never tested the app on the device it was designed for and will drag your app over the coals for doing this.

Steve was fascinated with a free iPad app that offered a fully functioning version of Microsoft Office in addition to cloud storage of documents on the popular Dropbox service. His fascination was quickly tempered by the fact that many of the Office UI elements were totally unusable on the iPad multitouch screen; they were simply too tiny for even small fingers to touch accurately. This is a perfect example of a potentially "killer" app being stymied by a poor user interface. He wanted so much to love this app; he did not.

Desktop apps should never migrate to the small screens of mobile devices without considerable thought as to how the user interacts with the app. Even more importantly, these apps should not be shipped without actual user testing taking place.

Refining the Product

Finish is a huge part of the product-review process. By "finish," we mean a completion of the development process—perfecting as many details as possible to create a product that feels refined and mature. You don't get second chances in reviewing. The product you deliver for evaluation is the one chance that product gets for its launch.

There are very, very few products that can live up to a philosophy of "we'll fix that feature later." The special products granted this exemption are unique. They are introducing something so ground-breakingly useful that reviewers will forgive any early imperfections. In most cases, bloggers will have been beating down your door asking, "Can we get early access to this?" In this case, and only this case, finish is excused.

In one case, a prototype power cord came apart in Erica's hands as she was working with a wall socket. It still got a positive write-up because we knew we were dealing with early access and the product itself was wicked cool. The manufacturer was apoplectically apologetic and sent over a box of t-shirts and hats, none of which we were allowed to keep. They were all given away.

For all other products, it's about spit and polish. We expect you to spend as much time tidying up loose ends, addressing small details, debugging and refining your product as you did developing it in the first place. If your instinct is to say, "Let's throw it out there and see how it does," we encourage you to stomp on that instinct—and stomp on it hard.

Products cannot find an audience without word of mouth, and few apps and accessories are so outstanding that people will forgive the rough edges of an early launch. Pushing to market too early dooms many promising products. If you cannot schedule in a testing period and user feedback along with time for product refinement, you have made a fundamental error in your business plan.

Consider scheduling a much longer testing period than you anticipate. Testing your product and fixing bugs always takes more time than you think. It's a good idea to have contingencies, both in time and money, in your project plan. Always build some padding into that plan, and you'll find that it's almost always never enough extra days and dollars to get all of your bugs worked out before shipping.

You cannot just say, "I'm bored developing now, let me see if I can earn a few bucks." Dev burnout is one of the biggest reasons we see so many unfinished uninspiring products cross our desk. It's an endurance race, not a sprint. That second half of the process, the fixing and finessing, is a crucial component to a successful launch. Turn the polishing part of your job into a fun process, perhaps giving yourself or your team rewards for achieving bug-smashing goals, and you'll be surprised at how an onerous task can become something your team wants to complete.

"Don't send in that 85%-done app. Don't send in an app that's just so-so. We don't want to review the same-old same-old that we've seen a thousand times before. Find your niche: be something different, or useful or fun. Your app doesn't have to be beautiful—it just has to be worth going back to over and over."

—Erica Sadun, TUAW Marketing LiveChat, January 2010

Beta Testing Your App

One good way to judge your market is to include potential users—and bloggers—in your testing. TestFlight (http://testflightapp.com) provides an amazing and free way to invite users to beta test your app and offer you feedback on what you're doing. Another such service is HockeyApp (http://www.hockeyapp.net/). For bloggers, it's a way to watch the app evolve from a rough idea to a polished gem.

Beta testing represents a critical part of any product development. It begins when your application or hardware is essentially feature complete, although most developers encourage users to make suggestions to add, expand, or alter features as they test. The point of beta testing is to find and eliminate bugs, to refine the user-facing interface, and to tweak the application for functionality based on user feedback.

In the past, we've been apt to write about apps we beta tested over those that we're totally unfamiliar with, because we feel invested in them. If the idea is good enough, you can ping us for interest even before you've gone beyond a prototype.

It's a pleasure to beta test exciting apps, but don't be surprised if a blogger declines the privilege. Unless there is something deeply compelling on offer, few bloggers have the time or (honestly) interest to beta test an app that's just like a hundred or a thousand other apps out there.

Erica: "Don't have your friends do your beta testing. Select picky OCD people who like to pick nits instead."

Steve: "I will often beta test apps for my clients, and I give them brutal feedback."

Erica: "Critical users are your best friends during testing."

—TUAW Marketing LiveChat (http://www.tuaw.com/2010/01/15/tuaw-livechat-promoting-your-app-store-products/), January 2010

Falling in Love with Your Product

Too often, developers become emotionally attached to their products, to the point that they can no longer objectively listen to the important criticism coming back from testers. There are features they "cannot" lose and functions they don't want to add. Essentially, this boils down to one core failure: forgetting about your audience and using yourself as the development litmus test.

If you are building products for some user base and you aren't responding to their feedback during testing, you're failing your product. When your users tell you that your product isn't hot and that it's not exciting, listen to them. You can convince yourself that you're building "the killer app," but it's not going to soar without a committed group of end users that are as passionate about your product as you are.

Development includes making hard decisions. Don't wait for your product to fail and for the inevitable post mortem to understand what features are broken. When testers offer criticism, listen.

Some feedback will be worthless; that's a basic reality of offering items for testing, but most feedback won't be. Pick your testers to best represent your eventual users, and then emotionally separate yourself from the feedback you're hearing. They are criticizing the product, not you.

A good developer treats negative feedback as a treasure, an opportunity to improve and grow a product, especially before launch.

NOTE

Avoid feature creep. Sometimes, developers think packing a product to the gills with functionality makes it more desirable. It does not. A product that does a job and does it well triumphs over a product that's overloaded with options. Less can be more, especially when less is clean and well designed and more feels cluttered and confusing. Feature creep can also kill project schedules; there's always "one more thing" (apologies to the late Steven P. Jobs) to add.

Nondisclosures, Embargoes, and Exclusives

Here's a basic rule of thumb: Don't ask bloggers to sign *nondisclosure agreements*. We don't have the money (out of our own pockets, no less) to hire lawyers to review NDAs, deciding if it's in our best interests to sign. We have lots of other work waiting for us. When it comes to basic cost/benefit analysis, NDA requests are one of the biggest red flags that suggest we should pick another project to write about.

Most bloggers are happy to keep things informally confidential. We call it the FriendDA (http://friendda.org/) principle. We'll keep mum about what you're developing, and you can keep us in the loop in advance of a release. If you don't trust a blogger enough to keep a FriendDA, this is probably not the person you want reviewing your product anyway.

We're used to honoring *embargoes*, a ban on publication until an agreed-upon date and time. Many developers prefer to launch a product across numerous sites at once to make the biggest splash. An embargo sets the date and time that blogs are allowed to push the Publish button. And, yes, we can and do mess up embargoes occasionally, but that's due to mistakes, not malice. Always be super clear—with short, easy-to-understand instructions—when requesting embargoed coverage. We won't be offended.

Be sure to let us know what time zone the embargoed time is based on. Many times, blogger confusion over whether it's 9 AM PST or 9 AM EST can be the cause of a blown embargo, as in the following case. The developer assumed we understood that he meant 9 AM Pacific Time. We posted it at 9 AM Eastern Time, the home time zone for our blog.

Please pull this story! That story was not supposed to get posted until after 9 AM, please pull it and 404 the page.

🎙 NOTE

There's a viral humor video (not safe for work; http://www.youtube.com/watch?v=IBCaS-Iz1_k) that has made a place in many bloggers' hearts that talks about honoring an embargo for eternity, thus never writing about the product, ever. This video also offers the classic line, "When every new social media service is revolutionary, it is no longer news," which is a basic blogging truth.

Do not offer a number of blogs the same embargo, and then allow one site to post information before everyone else. Nothing makes bloggers hate you faster than promising that everyone will hold the same embargo time and date, and then letting one favored site sneak out the information before everyone else. Trust us; bloggers have a long memory and will probably ignore you the next time you offer up information on your latest project.

Bloggers love *exclusives*. If you have developed a particularly good relationship with a specific site, you may want to offset your embargo to allow an exclusive launch on one site with coverage on other sites following. However, keep the following in mind: Unless your product is really big, important, or in demand, your exclusive offer won't merit consideration.

With exclusives and embargoes, make sure you specify exactly what terms you're looking for. At the same time, know that the more restrictions you put upon any idea, the less likely a blogger is to be interested in finding out more in the first place.

"It's not an exclusive when you send out the same information to every single blog on the 'net. Exclusive doesn't mean 'hot', 'worthy', or 'exciting.' It means a story published by only one source."

—Anonymous (ticked-off) blogger

🎙 **NOTE**

Do *not* renege on exclusives. Nothing angers bloggers like promising an exclusive and then seeing posts appear at the same time or (worse!) earlier on other sites. It's a great way to get your company blacklisted from future coverage. When providing exclusives, make sure you make yourself available for extra interview time, tech support, and so forth. You're essentially negotiating deeper coverage in exchange for exclusivity. Make it worth both your time and the blog's efforts.

Competing Against the Big Guys

We've mentioned apps that are big, important, and in demand, a.k.a premium apps. When Square Enix releases a new version of Final Fantasy for iOS or Facebook updates its official iPad software, we're going to be there and we're going to cover it—end of story. Few smaller developers possess the kind of sway with their apps that Rovio, Disney, and Halfbrick releases take for granted.

For most developers, the challenge is more about gaining market share and attention than managing popularity. They won't have to worry about fending off bloggers desperate to cover the latest, biggest, and most exciting small changes in an established brand. If you're reading this ebook, your product probably doesn't fall into the "premium app" category.

That means your strategy has to adapt itself accordingly.

The difference between reviews of the big-name products and indie ones comes down to passion. An indifferent update by a big developer will be covered, but it's probably going to be what we call a "quick hit." It lets people know that an update is available or a new software title has launched, and little else. We need to get it out, we need to get it out fast, and, well, that's usually about it.

Your product has to compete in this arena by finding its advocate, a blogger who appreciates it, who wants to promote it, and who offers a heartfelt endorsement of it. Bloggers love championing small, but overlooked, products. We're thrilled when an app or accessory we helped discover finds its audience and goes ballistic in sales.

Finding and promoting deserving products is a big part of blogging appeal. It's like going fishing and coming home with the 100-pound whopper that *didn't* get away. We experience a lot of broken hooks, mosquito bites, and angry sardines (free app idea!) along the way, but catching the big one is utterly addictive.

Blogs offer a great platform for small devs to compete against the big guys. If you have a worthy product and you can convince us to advocate for it, bloggers will be there to help launch and promote it.

Building in Self-Promotion

Bloggers are not the be-all or end-all of product promotion. Word of mouth and good product reviews play important roles for smaller devs. Your product should, as much as possible, help spread its own fame and encourage users to get the word out in a positive fashion.

Take some tips from premium products. Build your apps to do what the big guys do: leverage social networking and offer in-app review-nags. There's nothing shameful in doing so. At least there isn't if you add these tastefully and honorably.

Social networking helps promotes apps by creating a Posted From tag along with the app name and a status. Adding Twitter and Facebook buttons into your apps lets users post updates to well-trafficked sites. This lets people know that your app is being used and gives it exposure without spammy "I'm using Product X, you should, too" announcements. Be subtle; avoid the spam.

Use a reminder screen (one that's not *too* nagging) to encourage people to leave positive reviews. Your existing user base is a valuable resource, one that you should nurture. Request reviews only after your users have proved their loyalty.

Check first for repeated app use; this is fairly easy to program in. You can measure this by counting launches or tracking time spent in-app. Holding back on Please Rate this App screens until then offers a smart way to push reviews for only your most committed users.

Once past that threshold, encourage the users to point out what they like about your app. Also ask them to suggest features and improvements as part of their reviews. The more thoughtful the feedback, the more valuable it will be both to you and to potential purchasers. Asking for the bad as well as the good helps motivate users beyond the "ugh, I'm being spammed for stars" mentality and gives them encouragement to make the trip to the App Store review form. Do not offer free tote bags for 5-star reviews.

"I never read 1 star or 5 star reviews. A 2–4 star review means the reviewer thought more about it."

—Greg Hartstein

Always provide "Don't show this again" and/or "I've already rated the app" options. Some apps bug users even after they've left reviews. That's bad, karma-wise. Avoid ticking off your users wherever possible and don't forget to thank users for their effort if they choose the already-rated option. Perhaps consider a thank-you in the form of a free (to the user) in-app upgrade.

Sadly, you should not expect logic from most App Store reviewers. Anonymity means they tend to be a little more *id* and a lot less *superego* than on Amazon (speaking as writers, believe us when we say there's plenty of id on Amazon). Encouraging established loyal users to create reviews helps balance that skew.

"Chicken only had two drumsticks defying user expectations that everyone gets a drumstick. One star."

"Your app has not, to date, created world peace. One star."

"You said the tool box could be used for fixing stuff. I bought it. Nothing in my house got fixed. One star."

🎤 **NOTE**

No matter how much you love her, don't let your Mom review your app. "This is the best app ever! The developer is one smart cookie!" Astroturfing, the art of emulating a grassroots response by having friends, colleagues, and paid minions add fake positive reviews, doesn't go down well with purchasers or bloggers. Take the reviews that nature gives you. An orchestrated campaign is usually easy to detect and a quick sign that the app itself probably doesn't offer the actual value that its "users" are claiming.

Wrapping Up

In this chapter, you read about what makes products stand out and gain notice both in the marketplace and in a blogger's eyes. Here are a few final points to think about:

- Refinement is a key component of any attractive product. Even products with outstanding concepts rarely dazzle in their beta development. Test, tweak, and test some more. Make sure your product has the best possible finishing details before you ship.

- Listen to your product testers and target audience. They will have insights about using your product that you will never have on your own. If you haven't read any of Donald Norman's books (such as *The Design of Everyday Things*) or web articles on usability and designing for people (jnd. org), do that now.

- Never promise an exclusive to more than one blog. Just don't.

3

Crafting Your Pitch

Are you hoping that a blog will review your product? It's time to write a pitch and send it in. Pitches are a concise and compelling description of your product designed to stir up interest. A good pitch helps get the press buzzing about your work and opens the wallets of potential buyers. It's the bait you're putting on the virtual fishhook to reel in coverage and customers.

For blogs, the pitch introduces your product. It explains why the blog should devote time and resources to writing about it. In just a few lines, you have to introduce your product and motivate that potential reporting. Sadly, reality doesn't give you a lot of leeway in terms of getting to the point. You have to grab the blogger's attention and set up your product's story in a narrow time window before your email moves from the inbox to the trash bin.

Bloggers want to be sold by your passion. That passion needs to start in the subject line, which is the first thing they see. Your email should explain why bloggers should care and why they should be excited. Think as hard about these press materials as you do about the product itself. You want to create a message that is sharp and polished, and that presents the most compelling story possible about why your product will be interesting to their readership.

In this chapter, you learn about creating pitches that work and how to motivate that excitement.

Designing the Pitch

It's hard to market well. It is especially hard when you have neither a built-in bully pulpit like your own personal major blog and you don't have a lot of money to hire a professional marketing firm to get the word out. For most indie devs, that means going to websites and pitching solo, hoping you can sell bloggers on your passion and your product's basic quality. You basically want to tell as many websites as possible why your product is exciting. Unfortunately, many people do this very poorly.

The biggest problem is that you may have spent months, even years, developing this product. You love it. You have put your heart and soul into it, and then you spend two minutes to shoot an email off to a website like ours and your email reads, "Please review my product."

Here are some real-world review requests we've received over the last few weeks:

- Review
- Product review
- Submitting our app for review
- Please review my app
- I need a review
- Potential product review
- Kindle game review request
- Plz review
- App review
- iPhone Application Review
- Submission
- Be rewieved (sic)

When we get several hundred "Please review my product" emails every week, you can guess what's going to happen—yours will not stand out. There is a skill involved in successful pitching, one that is key to your success. The following section introduces the essential pitch components you need to include in your communication. If you've spent all those months working on your product, why are you spending just a few minutes on your pitch?

Essential Pitch Components

A good pitch contains many key ingredients. The secret is to provide all the essential ingredients without overwhelming your reader. Keep your style clean and to the point, but include each and every one of these items in your pitch, especially for software. If you're pitching hardware, you can adjust your submission accordingly.

A Motivating Subject Line

Subject lines are the elevator pitches of the blogging world. You have to jump in and motivate, define, and sell your product in 80 characters or less. A good subject line communicates the idea of the product and grabs the reader's attention.

Your subject should say *what* the product is, what *role* it plays, and how it *differentiates* itself from the competition. That may sound like a lot for such a small part of an email, but the subject line is the first thing potential reviewers see. It's got to get the message out there and establish why someone should care about the rest of the pitch.

Although daunting, it's possible to do all of this with just a few well-chosen words and phrases. Need some coaching? A full section about creating subject lines follows later in this chapter.

Product Name

Include your full product name, with exactly how you want it to be referred to and with proper spelling. You'd be surprised at how many times people ask us to review something and then forget to tell us its name. They say, "I have got a great video app, would you please review it?" and that's their entire pitch. Here's a real world example:

Subject: New iPhone Game

New game released yesterday. Please give it a look. Thanks

Don't forget the product name! Make sure it's the proper name, at that. Bloggers need the name that is used on the store, whether it's the Mac App Store, the iOS App Store, Google's Play Store, or if you're selling it through Amazon or whatever. Provide the full name with the proper spelling, capitalization, and punctuation, because that's what we use for the write-up.

It's also what we will use online to search for more background and details. We do searches once we get invested in doing a write-up, and the correct name matters. Reducing the hurdles you place in front of your reviewer helps encourage the product to be reviewed and published, especially in a world of tight deadlines where there's always another (easier) product waiting to meet a writer's quotas.

Product Price

We focus on iOS and Mac apps at our blogs, so we normally use the price from Apple's U.S. App Store in dollars. If the product or blog is specific to another region, such as Europe or Asia, specify both the region and the price in its local currency.

You wouldn't believe how many people forget to include how much a product costs and yet the price is a big part of the product story. If you're selling something for $39.99 versus $0.99, or $1,599 versus $749, that's telling us a lot about what this item is and its place within the competitive market.

Likewise, if you're marketing an app, and it is free for limited features but offers in-app purchases of expanded functionality, let bloggers know. Even something as simple as stating "free; in-app purchases available" or referring to your app as subscribing to the "freemium" model are clues to the blogging world that the app is pay-for-play.

We recently covered the Freedom Pop wireless router, which offers free high-speed Internet to consumers. Although its mobile units are "free," it does require a nearly $100 "deposit" to ensure their return, which becomes non-refundable after 1 year of use. This kind of non-price pricing is an important part of the cost story, so make sure that you include any financial details about your product that fall beyond the basic buy-then-use scenario.

Links

No matter what product you are selling, you need to include two links in your write-up. These URLs apply across the board. We want to see

- A link to your product's homepage on your own website. This may be an informational write-up page, such as http://mycompany.com/myproduct.aspx, or a primary product-related website, such as http://myproduct.com.
- A product purchase page, such as your own storefront/Buy Now, an Amazon listing, an App Store listing, and so forth.

The website link supports the blog write-up, allowing reviewers to read your app descriptions, find answers to FAQs, and more. The product purchase page appears in-article to provide a link for interested customers who want to place an order or download your app.

These URLs provide instant access to information that bloggers need, so they can jump directly there without having to start doing web searches. Be sure to check the links and their destination before sending your pitch; bloggers aren't fond of clicking links and being sent to a missing or incomplete web page (see Figure 3-1).

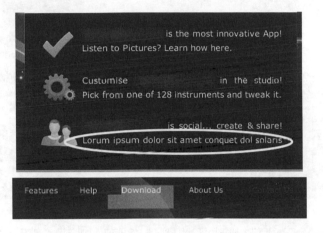

Figure 3-1
Placeholder text and nonfunctional links drive bloggers crazy when they're trying to prepare a write-up on short deadlines. Try to get your website up and running so the reviewer covering your product can do his or her research at your site.

Screenshots

Although you can include one or two screenshots in your email, do *not* overwhelm the reviewer with images. There's nothing quite like receiving a message that bombs your mailbox with too many pictures.

Instead, choose shots that highlight and explain your product. If you have more images to offer, provide a link to a press kit on your site. You may want to include pictures of your company's logo and your product at high resolutions as part of that press kit. Remember this: A few images help tell a story; too many of them create sensory overload.

Submit pictures that emphasize a compelling narrative. The left shot in Figure 3-2 showcases how an application uses Apple's wireless AirPlay service, a major selling point for the app. The right screenshot enumerates the social services the app supports. This latter uses a standard system-supplied sharing screen and falls into the category of "we've seen that" for anyone familiar with Apple's iOS world. If you have to choose between the two, always pick the image that offers the greater punch. In this case, the left image tells a much better story than the right. Your pitch would be better served by listing the supported social services rather than wasting one of your precious image slots.

Figure 3-2
Choose your pitch's product images carefully. Only send one or two pictures, and of those, select images that best showcase your product's features and GUI. In this example, the left image, with its more novel use case, does a better job telling this app's story than the right, with its system-supplied components.

 NOTE

Looking to create slicker product shots like the left image in Figure 3-2? The Promotee app ($4.99 for OS X) from Netwalk Apps lets you add screenshots to device templates, including iOS, Mac, and Android platforms.

Video

If a picture's worth a thousand words, then a video has to be worth at least a million. Videos help showcase your product in a quick, effective way that's invaluable to bloggers, especially for software. As a rule, always include a product video with your pitch. It need not be professional; it need not be well lit or brilliantly composed. Bloggers just want to see your product in action.

A video provides the quickest way to initially assess your product, letting us know if it's worth investigating further. If your pitch made us curious, your video can take us to the next step: committing to a product review.

We can't tell you how many times people have told us, "We'll have a video in a week. Do you mind waiting?" Make sure your video (even an amateur one) is ready before you send your pitches.

Here are a few tips about videos:

- **Short is okay**—A video doesn't have to be long. In fact, videos should be no longer than 30 seconds to 1 minute in length. Just shoot your product in-action. Thirty seconds plus a screenshot or two tells the story of the app. If you have a game you're working on, show us the game play. If it's an app doing time tracking, show us how easy it is to use. If it's a case, drop the phone. If it's a portable solar charger, show how it opens, closes, and fits into a backpack.

- **Amateur is okay**—We do not need or demand professional, well-lit, or well-composed videos. Honestly, we do not care about the glossiness. We just want to see it, and we just want to be able to initially assess the product. This is what tells us, "Is this app worth downloading?" or "Is this accessory worth testing further?" We just want to see what the product is about without having to download it or request a review unit.

- **Don't send the video file**—Send us a link to it instead. If you're worried about privacy, use YouTube's unpublished video feature, which allows you to set it up so only people you share the URL with can see it. Bloggers won't share that video unless you tell them it's okay.

Never underestimate the impact of a video. A short video tells us more about a product than any long-winded pitch description ever can. Use your pitch to convey your product's importance. Use the video to show us what the product is.

🎤 **NOTE**

Tips and how-to's for creating effective product videos follow later in this book.

Description

This is the heart of your pitch. Explain in one concise paragraph what your product does and why our readers should care. A good pitch describes and motivates, just like a good subject line, but it does so in greater depth. Explain what your product is, who its audience is, how the product works, and most importantly, what your product offers that sets it apart from the crowd. In essence, differentiate.

This differentiation is what sells your product both to blogs and your customer base. Think carefully as you develop and write these paragraphs. Focus on what your product does better, what it does differently, what it adds, and how it performs. Don't be wordy: a good description makes its points clearly and then stops before getting into too depth.

When describing what makes your product different, take care when calling out other products specifically by name. Don't be rude. Use positive well-sourced comparisons to show how your product trailblazes features and provides better service or reliability. If your feature set is truly exceptional, there's no need to compare it to other less worthy ones. It should shine on its own.

Additional paragraphs can update reviewers on what's changed since a previous release, plus *why* those changes were made. As a rule, however, if this information does not really add to the story you expressed in the first paragraph, we recommend skipping this.

TUAW blogger TJ Luoma offers the following recommendation on what makes a perfect software description for him:

First paragraph: Tell us what your app does. I'm amazed at how many people don't do this. Skip the overwrought adjectives about how "unique" and "innovative" your app is. Tell us what it does and why I should care.

Second paragraph: Tell me whatever is new assuming this isn't the first release, in case I tried it once and didn't like it. If it's a new app, tell me why you made it. What need did it fill? How does it change your life? What does it do that other, similar apps don't do?

Third paragraph: Tell me something I'm going to remember about you or the app. If this is your elevator pitch, my floor is approaching and the door is about to open. What do you want me to remember about you and the app?

Feature List

After describing your product, add a short but motivational feature list. Describe those features that make your product sparkle. Use bullet points to explain how your product stands out. These primary selling points should follow your description paragraph.

Try to include 5–7 points that highlight product functionality. Do not overwhelm bloggers with dozens of points. Keep your list focused and relevant. If your app truly is that special, sites will want to find out more after just a few points, which leads to the next part of your pitch.

Contact Information

Specify who you are and how to get back in touch with you. If you do not work directly for the development organization (e.g., you're sending this as part of a PR firm), make it very clear in the contact portion of your pitch. Your contact information is important to us, because we often need to coordinate with you during the product write-up.

Above all, include a working email address in your reply field. If you say you're "nope@sorry.com" (it's happened), bloggers will send your pitch to "notgoingtobe@reviewed.com." Typically, the rule is this: no valid email, no review.

Think we're kidding? See Figure 3-3. We sadly shake our head when we recall the missed opportunities developers have wasted, not to mention our lost time trying to pursue a review that didn't have a developer to stand behind it.

From: nope@sorry.com
Subject: [TUAW] TUAW - The Unofficial Apple Weblog
Date: July 26, 2011 11:11:55 AM MDT

Figure 3-3
Use a real email return address. Seriously.

A Sample Pitch

The list of pitch components you have just read through may sound like a huge amount to process. Despite that, each element plays an important role, providing key information. Together, these components aren't necessarily overlong. You're looking at about a single printed page of writing, all said. Here's what a pitch with all these components might look like:

Subject: Collage for iPad offers photo layout fun for parties and business meetings

Having a get-together at lunch, at a conference, or in the board room? Collage provides a quick, easy, and fun way to snap and arrange photos for instant event souvenirs. This app captures images with a single tap and uses the iPad's superb gesture control to rotate, resize, and lay out the pictures exactly the way you want. It takes just seconds to produce a one-of-a-kind collage of your event participants. Collage lets you:

• Add, delete, and reshoot images with simple touches.

• Interact with live video feeds in a preview photo that you manipulate.

• Choose from an assortment of background images, including granite, a corkboard, a blackboard, etc.

• Share by email, Twitter, Facebook, and more. Most popular social networks supported.

Collage ($2.99, iOS 6 and later) is available for sale now at the iTunes Store (link to iTunes). You can read more about it at my website (link to website). Here is a video of Collage in action: (link to video) and a couple of screenshots follow below. Want more information? Here's a full press kit for you to explore: (link to website).

Please feel free to contact me if you have any questions about the app, if you'd like a promo code for review, or to schedule a time to chat with me or my developers. My contact details follow. Thank you in advance for considering my app for review,

(Your contact info)

Notice each of the key components: a strong subject line, a summary paragraph, a short feature list, pricing, links, and contact information. This may sound like a lot of work, but it takes far less time than it did to develop your application in the first place.

To review, your pitch should contain:

- The exact name of your app, what it does, and why it is different
- The price you will be charging
- One link to your product page on your site and another to its iTunes product page
- One or two screenshots
- A link to a short video
- A concise description that specifies the audience, what the app does, and what sets it apart from the crowd
- Contact information

Remind Us Who You Are

Developers often forget how much information crosses a blogger's desk. There's a common error that many companies make, typically categorized as "we presume you have been following our product since birth." Start each new email thread with a bit of context. If you're replying to an email, that reply creates the context for you.

It is never a bad idea to include a brief product and company bio in your communication, reminding the recipient about your role in the world. If a site has covered your product before, include that, too. The quicker a blogger can come back up to speed on past coverage, the easier it will be to move forward to new events. It never hurts to assume that a blogger suffers from total or partial amnesia about your product and company.

Remember the movie Memento (http://www.imdb.com/title/tt0209144/)? The one whose leading man had anterograde amnesia? Treat your bloggers as if they were the Guy Pearce character in that movie. You don't have to tattoo your contact details on the bloggers' arms (in fact, we recommend against any forced blogger body mods as a rule), but it helps to start off each contact as if you needed to re-establish your existence in their world.

We may have met you at a conference. We may have spent time with you enjoying karaoke and Jello shots. But, there's still a good chance that when you ping us by email, a medium without faces or voices, that we'll have absolutely no idea who you are.

Here are a few quick pointers:

- Assume that bloggers suffer from total or partial amnesia about your product and who you are.
- Include a (brief!) company and product bio.
- Include links to past coverage from the site you're pitching to.
- Remind the site which blogger you worked with in the past.

Tell the blogger about your past interactions. ("Remember me? We were in that bathroom in Cupertino together when you had that stomach bug, and I offered you some Pepto as you were doing the Technicolor fountain." Or, "You did an amazing write-up of our product *AutoFixit Pro* last year, and I wanted to follow up about our newest offering.")

"Tell us who you are and what this product is first. Then, explain what's new and great, and do that in 75% fewer words."

—Victor Agreda, Jr., TUAW Editor-in-Chief

That's something I've had to put up with at Macworld for the last few years. People who come up and say "Hi. So, what do you think of our newest product?" and I'm looking at them like they're insane, because I have NO idea who the hell they are.

—Anonymous Apple blogger

Capturing Attention Through the Subject Line

Now that we've overwhelmed you with the structure of a pitch, it's time to step back a little, and go into the how's and why's in more depth. The next few sections slow down and introduce the pitch subject line in detail. Assuming you've hung in here and are now ready to explore these features, here are ways you can best build a subject line to create the greatest effect.

The Subject Line's Role

Pitching products establishes a relationship between yourself, your product, and the potential reviewer. When you pitch, you typically have just a few seconds to catch a reviewer's eye and make that person care about your product. Sites receive scores of pitches daily, not to mention PR blasts and personal emails. You need to make your pitch stand out. Bloggers want to find that next great app or accessory. A good subject helps them do that.

The very first thing bloggers see in their inbox is your subject line. Your subject introduces your product and explains why reviewers should be excited. A well-written subject gets straight to the point, announces the product, describes what it does, and says who it's for.

Expect your recipient to see no more than the subject line and possibly the first two lines of each email to determine what is worthy of additional attention—in other words, what you see when clicking through the inbox in Apple Mail. That sounds harsh, but when you realize that bloggers can sometimes go through a hundred or more pitches a day, it's not surprising.

Good Subject Lines

The following list provides good subject-line examples for made-up products. None of these examples are flawless, but they all work effectively. Always remember that perfection is the enemy of good. What you need for your pitch email is a good subject line, one that works to communicate your product's potential.

- New pirate game "Yar Har Algebra" teaches your kids math on the iPhone
- Ultimate Destroyer for Android blasts your way through outer space with high-powered explosions
- Compresso Plus's offsite compression reduces monthly data consumption *before* data reaches your computer or mobile device
- Calendar Superhelper: Organize your daily life more efficiently on Windows and OS X
- Watch any video format on your iPad, not just H.264, with Videoify for iPad
- Use your device up to 150% longer with Battery BoosTR's newly updated external USB power pack.
- Protect your laptop with the Basegio MiniShield. 100% of the protection, just 30% of the weight
- Jovana's SuperHUB 2™ powers all your 3.0 devices, adds 10W supercharging ports

These subject lines name the product, specify the platform they run on, and explain exactly what the product does. After looking through these, you know their genres immediately (education, gaming, telecom, etc.). What's more, you get a sense of the app's audience, be it kids, gamers, or general consumers.

Remember that many sites review apps for more than one platform. It helps to know that the *Calendar Superhelper* (for example) runs on OS X and Windows, not on iOS or Android. Don't be afraid of the extra characters. It doesn't take a lot to specify your app's target device.

Remember these points for good subject lines:

- Good subject lines communicate what a product does.
- They specify who the product is for, both audience and genre.
- They specify the platform that the product runs on.
- They provide a hook as to why a reviewer should be excited.

This last point, the hook, is both the most important and the hardest function to fulfill. It's a callback to your initial development analysis. There's a reason your product stands out from the competition. That reason belongs in your pitch subject line. Whether your product is different, better, more flexible, or more fun, your subject line should communicate that excitement.

Why Subject Lines Fail

Subject lines fail when they don't provide the information bloggers need to understand a product's who, what, and why. Here are examples of pitch subject lines that miss the mark, all adapted from real-world examples:

<no subject>—A completely missed opportunity.

Product review or **Please review this app**—What app is it? For whom? What does it do? These unadorned words in a subject line often cause an involuntary reflex in bloggers that causes the index finger to twitch and hit Delete.

Review our new puzzle game, Battle Snails *or* **Review our FUNKEH tablet case**—This is a better subject line, because it tells us what the product is and its name, but it doesn't explain the motivation, the genre, or the audience. You don't need to ask us to review your product. It's implicit in the fact that you're contacting us that you're trying to entice us to look at your app or hardware. Use those characters for a better purpose.

Pan-Fried Dumplings Free. Now available for iOS—This names an application and specifies the platform and what it costs, but does little in the way of promoting the software itself. Is it a cooking app? A game? An ebook? Sure, the name is intriguing, but it's not necessarily a motivation to read the rest of your pitch.

Promo codes for a new app *or* **Review unit available**—Everyone loves trying out products, but this subject doesn't specify what product you're writing about or any other hook. For apps, there's a good chance that you just wasted the promo codes you sent. Bloggers see so many offers for app promo codes that they're just not that much of an enticement as many developers hope.

Each of these subject lines fail because they're not specific or motivational. Their generic nature means they won't catch a blogger's eye and make them pay attention. Recall the key rules for good subjects discussed earlier in this chapter. You should

- Name the product.
- Motivate the product with a hook, something designed to catch people's attention.
- Specify the platform(s) the product works with.

Each of these sample subjects failed to provide one or more of these key points. In doing so, they flopped in explaining their product to bloggers. A pitch that doesn't make a blogger want to open the email and read about the product in more depth is a failed pitch. Bad subject lines are typified in the following ways:

- Bad pitches don't explain the who, what, and why of the product.
- Bad pitches are not specific or motivational.
- Bad pitches don't name the product or specify a platform(s) it's used with.
- Bad pitches don't provide a hook.

🎙 **NOTE**

Always specify your platform even for iOS- or Android-specific sites. This especially holds true when your app only works with phone features (so can't be used on tablets) or is meant just for some members of the covered computing family.

Subjects for Non-Review Pitches

Many developers think that they only way they can solicit coverage for their products is to solicit a review. They couldn't be more wrong. Blogs cover lots of stories. Reviews only make up a small portion of those write-ups. Blogs also post about updates, sales, items in the news, and more.

Your subject lines shouldn't be limited to new review pitches, either. Each of the following subject lines offers a coverage opportunity that goes beyond a simple "review this product" request:

- Blingo for OS X: Best audio editor now supports export to five new formats
- Top-rated Android first person shooter Biffy Goes Wild goes free for Halloween Weekend
- Black Friday Special: Hubitorium offering 25% discount to TUAW readers
- Fan favorite virtual aquarium app Swimmy for iOS acquired by Snippet Games
- MaxiDrive SSD pricing now 20% lower; capacity increased to 800 GB
- Hurricane Lessons: BackupPro and the importance of offsite backups

These provide examples of other real-world situations where you may email a site to promote your product. You might introduce a major update, put your product on sale, or announce a corporate event that affects your title. Sites are often interested in these events as well as items for potential review.

Always try to think of what makes your products or business newsy. If you can tie your app, hardware, or company into a story that could be featured on major blogs, go ahead and pitch it. It may not make the cut, but unless you put it out there as a potential story, it can't be considered in the first place.

You don't want to overwhelm bloggers with minutia of your day-to-day business practices, but if you think major app update or personnel changes deserve wider attention, go ahead and put those facts out there through press releases and blog pitches.

Promo Codes

Promotional (promo) codes are a feature that allows you to gift free review copies of intangible products to bloggers (see Figure 3-4). You'll find these used for books and applications in many stores. We work in the Apple world, so we commonly handle promo codes from the iOS and OS X App Stores, as well as from Apple's iBookstore. We also occasionally receive Amazon gift certificates and product codes to use at O'Reilly Media, Apress, and other publishers.

Redeem Code   🔒 Secure Connection

Enter your Gift Card or Download Code:

KL04MQH3PXM1   Redeem

Give a Gift on iTunes ›

Figure 3-4
Promo codes and gift cards allow reviewers to purchase intangible products for testing.

As a rule, pretty much every website you ask will say, "You don't have to send promo codes." We will ask for them if we're interested in looking over your application or book. Apple offers 50 promo codes per app product release. If you update your app, you get 50 more codes. You can also gift applications, paying just 30% of the application price because you receive 70% of the sale back from Apple.

So, should you include promo codes or gift cards in your book or application pitches? We're going to answer this, but we are *not* doing so in any official capacity. This is not any website's policy, and we are *not* trying to tell you what you must do.

So, what is our answer? It's this: Don't bother sending unsolicited gift cards. We'll return them or toss the email without seeing the redemption code, and you'll be out of some money. Promo codes are a different matter. We understand that Apple developers and authors receive 50 units for free.

We believe if you are a relatively unknown developer, you'd be foolish not to include a promo code for your application with your pitch. That promo code helps you leverage what we can only call "blogger curiosity". Offering a promo code opens the door to a blogger's impulse to try out new things.

Bloggers often cash in promo codes just to see what the app is like. If they have time to play around and the app sounds even the slightest bit interesting, they may simply throw the code into iTunes to see if there's anything worthwhile there.

These are the same bloggers who will likely not write back because they don't want to waste one of your promo codes and don't want to promise you a review. Remember: We're human. We feel awkward asking for things, especially when we can't make you any promises about using it. Including promo codes help you skip the bit where the blogger has to write back. You offer the code, you give them the option of using it or not using it, and the story ends there.

In our experience, a promo code doesn't guarantee anything. It just opens the door ever-so-slightly wider, making it easier for the blogger to look at your app. Anything that removes obstacles between the blogger and the actual app experience will serve your interests.

Yes, the promo code may go stale. And yes, the blogger may download your app and then a few weeks or months later delete it without ever actually using your app, but this is a better chance at a review than having your pitch immediately go into the "meh" pile.

Do not include a promo code because you must or you ought; do it out of self-interest. Do it because it helps increase your odds, however small, for that all-important review.

🎙 NOTE

All promo codes have an expiration date and can only be used before that date, four weeks after the date of issue. Apple promo codes are available for Mac and iOS applications and iBooks. You must enter into a separate Promo Code agreement with Apple when you place your request. You may request a maximum of 50 codes per app version or book release.

How to Send Promo Codes

The simplest way to share a promo code with a blogger is to paste it directly into an email. If you know the date the code was created and when it will expire, add that information as it is valuable to the recipient (e.g., *issued 4/05, expires 5/05*).

That's because bloggers often return to older pitches they marked for later review. Knowing if a promo code is still valid removes obstacles on the path to their redemption. This is particularly valuable information when bloggers decide whether to investigate further and need to weigh how much work will be involved.

Some developers choose to send a redemption link instead of a basic promo code. Links allow reviewers to click-and-redeem as a single action. (This is great when the redemption request works, and not so great if it doesn't.) We recommend always including the actual code along with the link as a procedural backup.

A basic redemption link looks like the following, with the actual code appended to the end instead of the words "promocode." This link opens in a web browser and then redirects redemption to iTunes:

https://phobos.apple.com/WebObjects/MZFinance.woa/wa/freeProductCodeWizard?code= promocode

If you have the skills, you can create a more indirect link that goes through a website, issues a promo code, and tracks its redemption. Although still relatively rare, some of the vendors we work with have started doing this as a way of better monitoring code use. (How-to is left as an exercise for the reader.)

Creating a Product Link

In the Apple world, it's easy to copy an iTunes link. Right-click the app icon and choose Copy Link from the pop-up. The link is saved to the system clipboard, ready to be pasted into your pitch email. For Google Play, just right-click and copy the link from your favorite browser. (See Figure 3-5.)

Figure 3-5
Copying product links for your pitches.

For developers with products in the Amazon App Store, open your app's page in the store. In your browser's address bar is a long form address that looks like this:

http://www.amazon.com/Imangi-Studios-LLC-Temple-Run/dp/B00B2V66VS/ ref=sr_1_1?s=mobile-apps&ie=UTF8&qid=1360692405&sr=1-1

Delete all of the information after the last forward slash and you get a much more manageable URL that still works perfectly:

http://www.amazon.com/Imangi-Studios-LLC-Temple-Run/dp/B00B2V66VS/

Creating a Company Link

You can also create company links for your app-related communications. These links point to all of your company's products in a store, not just individual apps. In the Google Play store, click the developer's name, and then copy the company-specific URL (for example https://play.google.com/store/apps/developer?id=Disney).

Because Apple does commerce through iTunes rather than the web, it offers an interactive web tool to help with this. To create an "artist link," as these are called, point your browser to itunes.apple.com/linkmaker and enter your company name in the Search field (see Figure 3-6, left). Set the country and Media Type and click Search.

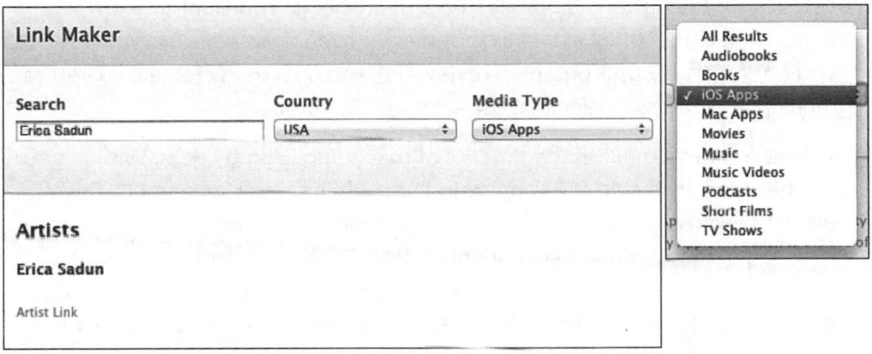

Figure 3-6
Apple's Link Maker is found at http://itunes.apple.com/linkmaker.

The newly generated link appears below as Artist Link, along with a list of the apps found In the requested country store that match your search term. Right-click and copy the link to your system clipboard (see Figure 3-6, right). Erica's artist link is itunes.apple.com/us/artist/erica-sadun/id282772077.

You can use this link maker to create artist links for the iOS app store, the Mac store, and iBooks. Because links are generated on a country-by-country basis, you'll usually want to make sure the link you send matches the home country of the blog you're communicating with.

A Genre/Category option on the Link Maker page lets you limit searches to Games, Utilities, and other categories. Use this option when you have a lot of content on the store and want to narrow the search results to a specific product type.

Tokens for Mac

For iOS and OS X developers, we recommend Tokens for Mac ($29, usetokens. com). It helps you track and manage your available promo codes. Keeping on top of your promo codes can be a hassle. Most developers end up with text files by the dozen or complicated spreadsheets. You want to know when items were issued (they expire in four weeks), who they were shared with (so you can follow up with potential reviewers), and how many remain so you can manage the 50 codes allocated for each app revision.

Tokens for Mac simplifies the process of managing promo codes. With it, you can generate trackable codes that ping you when they're redeemed. To start using the software, just sign in to iTunes Connect. From there, Tokens takes over and manages the process of contacting Apple and retrieving product info. Because the app is basically scraping the App Store, its use falls outside the Mac App Store guidelines. You need to purchase the utility directly from the developer.

Tokens starts by showing you a list of all your apps once you've signed in. You immediately see the remaining available promo code slots, which are shown as "available." (See Figure 3-7, left.) Upon choosing a code to redeem, Tokens requests it from iTunes, signs the contracts for you (a convenience I find amusing, which you may too if you think about it for a few seconds), and downloads the code. You're now ready to share it.

To share, Tokens creates an interactive webpage link (see Figure 3-7, right) that tracks redemption and offers a one-click solution for reviewers.

Figure 3-7
Tokens for Mac helps iOS and OS X developers manage their promo codes.

Going Free

If you're an application developer in the Apple ecosystem, you may want to consider an alternative to those 50 promo codes. Instead of using up codes at launch, consider making your app free for a while. It's a great way to allow reviewers to download your app without restriction and create some buzz, all at once.

A free promotional period can drive your launch, building momentum as the app first debuts. This same approach can be used with books at Amazon, through Amazon's exclusive KDP Select program. You can select up to 5 free days every 3 months.

Free's not just about launch, however. Going free provides a way to give your app a "second chance" at reviews it may have missed out on during your initial release.

Any short free period helps promote your product by raising its rank and visibility in its store. Your goal is to create enough awareness that word-of-mouth and rankings will help propel sales once the product returns to its paid status.

Hi there. I just wanted to let you know that [Product Name], the addictive puzzle game for iPhone and iPad is free for the next couple days. We are currently ranked in the top 25 of puzzle apps and top 10 of trivia apps and rising. I'd love to get a mention on your website. We were mentioned on both Engadget.com and Appadvice.com today. Our link is itunes. com/apps/productname.

THANK YOU,

James

Differences Between Hardware and Software Pitches

As the hardware editor for TUAW, Steve not only sees various PR blasts for software, but he's also the recipient of hundreds of emails touting the latest cases, hard drives, styluses, microphones, and other products for Apple gear.

In many ways, it's easier for someone to write a hardware pitch, because there are usually physical or performance parameters that make one product stand out over another. There are also non-measurable criteria that make certain products worth reviewing, most dealing with new hardware categories (spudgers, anyone?) or outstanding design.

Most of the focus in hardware reviews goes toward three criteria: *design*, *value*, and *functionality*. Highlight these focus points in any pitch you create to excite bloggers about reviewing your device.

Design

For many accessory items, *design* represents one of the key features that differentiate your product from the competition. For example, Steve receives a lot of iPad cases to review. Just looking around his office at this point in time, you can see 13 different cases, most of which look remarkably alike.

If your product looks more *stylish* than the rest, point that out in your pitch. One of the most memorable iPad cases Steve has ever reviewed (http://www. tuaw.com/2011/11/07/fu-design-lettre-x-robot-99-special-edition-the-coolest-ipad-2/) wasn't that hot in terms of build quality or functionality, but it did have an amazing cartoon-like design on the outside (see Figure 3-8). That resonated with Steve's childlike 55-year-old mind, and it got attention where a more mundane and businesslike case would have gone right into the email trashcan.

Figure 3-8
A beautiful iPad case.

One "me too" product that is pitched to TUAW on a way-too-frequent basis is the iPad keyboard case. Most of them are way too thick, have lousy keyboards, or, sadly, both.

When accessory manufacturer Logitech shipped one that was not only incredibly thin but was also touted by other reviewers as having a great keyboard feel, Steve got excited and asked Logitech's PR firm for a review unit. The keyboard cover that arrived in a few days did not disappoint. Steve's review reflected his excitement about how it looked and worked. That's what good design will do for a blogger.

Know your potential audience, too. At TUAW, we focus on Apple products, so we know what excites our readers. Steve has written reviews for clear polycarbonate desk mounts for the Mac mini, simply because of the unique design and its application to an Apple device. A major external disk-drive manufacturer got a good review from TUAW for a disk drive that is specifically designed as a perfect companion for a present-day Apple iMac. Once again, a design feature made just enough difference for me to consider the drive worth writing about.

Value

We've mentioned the importance of value to blog readers elsewhere in this book, and it is equally important when discussing hardware and accessories. *Value* doesn't necessarily mean "cheap;" it *does* mean that the product provides more bang for the buck in terms of design or functionality than its competitors.

Value is represented by emotional reception to a product compared to its price. Your product has to deliver something that's worth at least—and hopefully more—than its sticker price, at least in the customer's perception.

Potential customers want value, especially in times of economic hardship. It's important when you're selling a 99¢ app; it's absolutely *crucial* when you're trying to get a customer to buy a $99 iPad case.

The words "solid," "well-built," and "useful" all speak to how people perceive value. Customers will pay more for better quality, but they want to feel they've paid a fair price in return. That trade-off between cost and utility is how we evaluate value for our readers.

Functionality

One key criterion Steve uses to make the decision of whether or not to write about a new piece of hardware is *functionality*. Does the hardware or accessory provide a new function that hasn't been available up until now? Does it make performing a specific function easier to accomplish? Does it do it faster, with less user involvement? Are fewer cables involved, or can the new hardware provide wired capability over radio frequencies? Is it more energy efficient, or does it use a form of renewable energy?

The functionality of a hardware product is so important that a manufacturer who is pitching a product must first talk about function. An example of how functionality can get your foot in the door at a blog came up soon after the third-generation iPad showed up. There was talk about how the higher amperage requirements for charging made some third-party charging cables and accessories unusable with the new iPad. One manufacturer pinged Steve with a pitch about an in-car charger that could actually charge two of the third-generation iPads at the same time, so he jumped on doing a review.

The moral? Be aware of issues that are occurring in the marketplace, and if your product is able to surmount those issues, you've got a great pitch for a story.

Hardware Pricing

There is one more thing to remember about hardware reviews: Not only are they much more likely to be written, but there aren't as many hardware products as there are apps, and they are much more apt to receive attention from blog readers. It's not uncommon for someone to drop a buck or two on an app that looks interesting, only to toss the app after trying it out. The situation is different when a person can be looking at spending a significant amount of money on a hardware purchase.

Particularly for very expensive hardware that you're pitching to bloggers, be sure to give them some compelling reasons why people should buy your accessory or equipment. When bloggers have seen a bunch of sub-$100 iPad keyboard cases, tell them what makes your $199 case special enough to merit spending twice the amount of money to purchase it. They're not the only people who want to know; the readers are going to question equipment that seems to offer similar functionality at a much higher price. By "question," we mean that they're going to question your sanity and motives in the comments on the blog.

NOTE

With accessories, never forget what percentage of purchase price your hardware represents. Our readers are well aware that a $100 keyboard for a $400 tablet accounts for a 25% boost in monetary investment.

Video Gold

If there's one suggestion we can make to those who are pitching a physical product to bloggers, it's to make sure that you have a product video. In some cases, it helps clarify some questions that the blogger has about your product, but for the most part, it's there to show all the physical attributes of your product before you actually send out review hardware.

It doesn't take much skill, time, or money to create an effective marketing video. We've been sent videos that were shot and edited on an iPhone using iMovie for iOS, and they've been tremendously effective. Stock music and titles can tell the story faster and more professionally than a bad voiceover, so don't think that you need to hire a voice actor or record your own voice.

As with apps, marketing videos help us understand the product quickly and see how they're used in the real world. Keep the video short (30–60 seconds is ideal), keep your camera in focus, and remember that you're trying to communicate and sell. Share the ways your product can be used in real life.

For a good idea of what to do and not do with product videos, think of some of your favorite tech products and then see if you can find manufacturer videos out on YouTube. Watch a few of them, and take notes on which ones you like and those that turn you off. It doesn't take a lot of time to do this, and a little bit of homework can help you learn how to make an effective product video.

Hardware Review Logistics

Hardware is generally more expensive than the average app, so when a blogger asks for review equipment, he or she usually plans to write about it. Due to the expense involved in shipping hardware, don't send it to the blogger unsolicited. If we decide not to write a review, you're not only going to be out the cost of the hardware, but you'll also pay for the shipping.

For really expensive equipment, like RAID arrays or computer equipment, be sure to ask the blogger to return the equipment. In a case like this, it is generally accepted practice to include a return shipping label and a cover letter letting the blogger know that he or she needs to return the equipment within a certain time period.

Steve had a personally embarrassing situation occur one time where a manufacturer sent an interesting accessory for a review, but said nothing about returning the accessory when he was done with it. After several months, he included it in a box full of giveaway equipment that was sent to New York City for a TUAW meetup. About a month after the meetup, Steve received an email from the manufacturer asking when he'd be sending back the accessory. That was awkward, to say the least.

Most reputable blogs refuse to keep the review hardware, instead offering it to readers in giveaways or donating it to worthwhile causes. Why? Blogs do not want to create the appearance of exchanging reviews for payment of any kind. Providing review hardware as a giveaway item for a blog is a great way to build goodwill not only with bloggers, but to also get readers excited about your product.

There are some exceptions to the giveaway rule, however. Examples include earbuds that become encrusted with blogger earwax during review (something that is unsanitary, rather disgusting, and actually quite common), clothing items, or items that become damaged during the review.

If you want reviewers to return cables, specially designed twist-ties (not a joke), and other smaller pieces, make it clear in the letter to the reviewer that you place in the box along with the product. Many companies request only the return of the primary item, assuming it will be completely cleaned up and repackaged for the next reviewer so it arrives pristinely as the manufacturer ships it.

During unboxing, it's common for small items to be lost and the packaging to be destroyed. If these items are important to you, state so explicitly. We've had incidents where panicked PR representatives have contacted us asking, "Where's the tiny microphone that was included in the packaging" that we missed entirely and that was accidentally tossed with other post-review paraphernalia, such as packing pellets, warranty cards, and so forth.

Especially for larger items, it's generally courteous to include a return-shipping label along with re-packaging instructions to make it easier for reviewers to return your equipment after the review. Most sites can ship items back on their own dime, but they'd prefer not to.

Benchmarks

When you send hardware to a blogger that can be physically compared to other competing products, expect that the hardware is going to be benchmarked against similar equipment. Receiving benchmark information from companies is rather suspect; Steve would rather perform his own tests and comparisons instead of relying on numbers provided by manufacturers. On the other hand, if you can provide bloggers with benchmarks from an independent tester, that is definitely acceptable.

Note that bloggers can run into issues when performing their own benchmark tests. Steve ran a series of tests on a portable RAID array from a reputable manufacturer and found that the array ran slower as a RAID 0 striped set than as a RAID 1 mirrored set—something completely contrary to what should normally happen. He noted that discrepancy in his review and almost immediately received concerned feedback from the manufacturer, who pointed out that other benchmarking software showed proper results and that his computer's FireWire 800 port might be faulty. Needless to say, Steve updated the review with the manufacturer's comments and began looking for another way to test FireWire drives.

Other benchmarks rely on more subjective tests. When asked to review headphones, earphones, or speakers, Steve always prefaces his comments with a note stating that the sound quality he writes about might be affected by personal listening preferences. Anyone providing sound equipment to reviewers might want to include more objective evidence, such as frequency response charts or reviews from audiophile magazines.

🎙 **NOTE**

During reviews of headsets, speaker phone docks, or telephony software, for example, we may place calls to other bloggers on our team to hear their (subjective) feedback about audio quality. We try to include their comments about crackling, clipping, lags, and other unwanted effects into our write-ups.

A Word About Kickstarter

Creating hardware can take a lot of time and money. For something as simple as a phone or tablet case, a manufacturer may need to pay for CAD assistance, 3D printing to make a usable prototype, development of a master mold, and more. All that work burns cash, which is why a lot of folks working on hardware projects are looking for funding on Kickstarter (http://kickstarter.com).

Kickstarter is a wonderful way to do three things: get out the word about your potential product, get funding to pay for development of the product, and weed out product ideas that aren't going to be successful.

As a result, bloggers receive a *lot* of pitches for Kickstarter projects. Although this is a great way to excite potential customers about your future plans for a product, you also have to sell a blogger on writing a post about a product that may or may not make it to market. That's even tougher than getting them to write about a product that's ready to sell.

Here are a few suggestions about pitching Kickstarter projects:

- Don't try to get bloggers involved unless it appears that your project is actually going to be funded by the deadline date.
- Don't create a desperation bid to get publicity if you have a week to go and your project is only 25% funded.
- Don't call or write us with amazing stories about your new product idea that hasn't even been accepted by Kickstarter.
- Don't ask all of your friends and colleagues to write us to kick off a fake "grass roots" campaign for your Kickstarter project.

Finally, remember this: Bloggers are not a source for establishing venture-funding angel relationships for you. Again, this may come across as harsh, but it's a basic fact of blogging life.

Case Study: The Une Bobine Video

Kickstarter depends on a short video to tell the story of a potential product, and those videos are what capture or release our attention. Want an example of a good pitch video for Kickstarter?

Look at the "trailers" for Une Bobine, which is a simple spring-like iPhone stand and connector (see Figure 3-9) (http://www.kickstarter.com/projects/382469225/une-bobine-for-people-who-love-iphone).

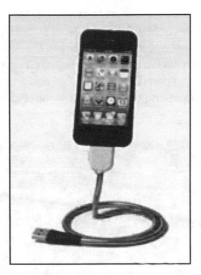

Figure 3-9
Une Bobine was a beautifully designed iPhone stand and connector that really got us excited.

These were created using iMovie and use a combination of the built-in trailer templates and some hand-drawn stick figure animation—all done on an iPad—to tell a story that was compelling and humorous. That's one way to get the attention of a blogger!

While the creator of Une Bobine initially had no samples that he could provide for a review, Steve was intrigued enough by the design and amused enough by the videos that he featured them on a weekly video podcast for TUAW. Although the product had already reached its funding goals, that extra bit of publicity helped Une Bobine gain even more backers.

Common Hardware Product Categories

This section walks through some of the more common product categories for hardware and accessories and provides some tips on what features you might want to focus on when pinging your favorite bloggers to write a review or highlight post.

Cases

To really get a blogger's attention and actually get him to write a decent review, an iPad, iPhone, or Mac case must have an outstanding design feature. This is perhaps the most overloaded category in the Apple accessory world, and there are so many similar cases out there that it's easy to ignore your pitch. Want to see just a part of the pile of iPad and iPhone cases Steve has on hand for review while writing this book? Check out Figure 3-10.

Figure 3-10
That's a *lot* of cases.

To make an impact, show pictures of what makes your product stand out in the crowd or give details about a different functionality that no one else has. Otherwise, a blogger's finger will quickly move to the Delete button.

Some examples of cases that have recently caught Steve's attention include an iPad case that is imprinted with your own photography, an iPad backpack (the iBackFlip Somersault; http://ibackflip.com/shop/ibackflip-somersault/)

that turns into a support for using the tablet while standing up, and a series of whimsically designed iPhone cases that each feature a unique texture design on the outside of the case.

Headphones/Earphones

As noted earlier, this is a place where a lot of review results are completely subjective and depend on the reviewer's hearing and emotional response to music. We get a lot of me-too products in this area, so functionality differences are what bloggers want to hear about.

Steve enjoyed reviewing CordCruncher (http://www.kickstarter.com/projects/1587181400/cordcruncher-earbud-headphones?ref=live), which is a set of earbuds that use a unique sleeve over the cables to keep them from tangling (see Figure 3-11). In terms of sound quality, the noise-cancelling headphones from Able Planet (http://www.ableplanet.com/) are totally beyond anything Steve's used before, so they were a pleasure to review. A Kickstarter project for a pair of earbuds that also allow you to hear ambient noises and avoid getting hit by a car (AIRBudz; http://www.kickstarter.com/projects/1415303287/airbudz?ref=live) definitely got our attention.

Figure 3-11
The CordCruncher keeps cables from tangling.

Docks

In this category, it's all about design and integration with devices. An attractive design, however, can only make up so much ground if the dock is poorly integrated with the target device.

As an example, some docks come with apps which, once installed, provide full control of the dock. This can be useful when using the dock as an alarm clock, using it to provide a musical or sound interlude before sleep, or controlling a built-in FM radio. Watch the design, too. Steve recently reviewed a Tick Tock Dock alarm dock with a time display that was completely obscured by the docked device (http://www.tuaw.com/2012/04/13/a-pair-o-docks-edifier-tick-tock-dock-and-xtrememac-luna-voyag/) (see Figure 3-12). Needless to say, that had Steve scratching his head for a while, wondering what the designers were thinking.

Figure 3-12
When the iPhone is inserted, as designed, it hides the clock display. What *were* those designers thinking?

Speakers

Bluetooth speakers are a popular hardware accessory category. Things to point out to possible reviewers include battery life, ease of charging, ability to withstand impact or splashes, and overall volume. Make sure that your product requires little or no time to pair with a handheld device, and you'll make me—and your customers—happy.

You'd think that there's not a lot you could do with the design of a Bluetooth speaker, and you'd be wrong. Design is, once again, a product differentiator in this category, and an attractive design gets our attention much faster than a plain grey box. On TUAW, we've recently reviewed Bluetooth speakers that attach to a bicycle or helmet, and devices that convert any speakers for Bluetooth readiness.

Drives

In a world where most hard drives are manufactured by the same handful of companies, it all boils down to design and functionality. External drives that complement the equipment they're designed to work with are going to be attention-getters, and size and speed are always considerations to look at for mobile equipment. Consider the Iomega eGo Helium, as shown in Figure 3-13. It's small, lightweight, and offers a huge capacity for storage.

Figure 3-13
The Iomega eGo Helium offers portable storage.

Remember that reviewers are not always going to have the latest computers available for testing (at least not at our blog, where we provide our own equipment), so when a new interface like Thunderbolt becomes available, it may be difficult for you to get reviews. In cases like this, consider doing side-by-side video comparisons showing just how fast the new devices are so that you can impress the blogger without having to send him a loaner computer for testing.

In fact, Steve had to recently send off a drive to Erica for testing. She was already using a new 2012 Mac mini, complete with USB 3 ports, while he had to wait for his new iMac to ship.

Power Supplies (Batteries, Chargers, Car Chargers)

Another popular accessory category has grown up around the need for our devices to outlive the limited battery capacity they're designed with. Whether it's an external battery pack, a charger that connects to a wall outlet, a solar charger like the Eton Mobius (see Figure 3-14), or a dual-outlet adapter for a car, power supplies are something that people need.

Figure 3-14
People love solar chargers for emergency power, especially during disaster situations, like Hurricane Sande, we mean, Hurricane Sandy, which hit the Eastern U.S. in late 2012.

It's easy for manufacturers to toss out carbon-copy equipment that won't attract the attention of bloggers. What are we looking for? Alternative energy sources, like solar panels or fuel cells, devices that use less energy while charging devices faster, or multitaskers, like a combo spare battery/data sync cable/SD card reader.

As with all the other hardware and accessory categories listed here, give bloggers the special features up front to catch their attention.

Camera Accessories

The excellent cameras in our handheld devices have become the source of another category of accessories. These come in different flavors: accessory lenses that change the field of view (like the Photojojo lens pictured in Figure 3-15, stands to help hold the phone or tablet in place for better photographs) and devices that make it easier to take photos, like "big buttons" or camera remotes.

Bloggers want to see the end result of your product, so here's a situation where a review device can really help out. Don't send one unannounced, however; make sure that the blogger is interested first. This is another area where a product video can get the point across to a blogger, showing how the device works to improve "iPhoneography" or make it easier to take good pictures.

Figure 3-15
iPhoneography, as we call it, is a big review area for us.

Books/Ebooks

If you're pitching a book or ebook to a blogger, know your audience. We often receive emails from publishers who send out review requests for books that have nothing to do with our blog's focus. We're unlikely to write about making Lego weapons when we're focused on the Apple market (see Figure 3-16).

Likewise, it is foolish for a publisher to pitch a book on iOS development to an Android site, yet according to my compatriots at a few Android-centric blogs, they frequently receive this type of pitch. Think before you send!

Figure 3-16
Books may, or may not, be appropriate for blog reviews. Erica regularly covers books on Mac/iOS development and general use on her TUAW Bookshelf write-ups.

Cables and Gizmos

Even an item as mundane as a cable or a cord wrap can be worth writing about, provided that it shows design or function that's out of the ordinary. Take, for example, the first pitch we received from crowdsourced design firm Quirky (http://www.quirky.com/). It was for the PowerCurl, a cord wrap that fits around the power adapter for Apple's MacBook line of notebook computers.

The pitch included a photo of the brightly colored PowerCurl (http://www.quirky.com/products/15-PowerCurl-Mac-Cord-Manager) (see Figure 3-17), a list of the benefits of the device, and a description of how Quirky works to design and perfect different consumer products. The PowerCurl was insanely simple, yet something no one else had ever created. We not only wrote a review of the device, but Steve bought one for personal use and has also become a Quirky participant.

Figure 3-17
The PowerCurl combined utility with beautiful design.

Likewise, a product that fits a niche can excite a blogger. A recent case in point is the Kanex ATV Pro (http://www.kanexlive.com/atvpro), a dongle that makes the missing connection between an Apple TV box and a PC projector. The Apple TV uses HDMI for a connection to an HDTV, so it can't be used out of the box with the vast majority of projectors.

Kanex created a box that connects to the Apple TV on one end, and has a standard VGA connector on the other end to hook up to the projector. The result? Anyone can now use AirPlay to beam presentations from an iOS device to a projector.

It's something that was so obvious that a lot of bloggers wondered why no one had stepped up to the plate and delivered the product. It really got the attention of several bloggers at TUAW, who give presentations on a regular basis.

Hardware Pitches

Pitching hardware or an accessory to a blogger takes as much skill as trying to get a writer interested in an app. In some cases, it can be even more difficult because of the commodity nature of accessories, like smartphone cases.

When you're writing a pitch for hardware or accessories, remember that a blogger wants to see what's new or different about your product in terms of design, functionality, and value. Sending out a generic release about another iPhone case that looks just like a thousand other cases won't result in a blog post. As in the case of creating an app, your product's ultimate success should be in mind before you start designing it.

Because a good part of your marketing depends on the kindness of bloggers, don't do yourself a disfavor by trying to sell a crappy product. Create something new, different, and good, and the world will beat a path to your door, after they've read about you on a blog.

Wrapping Up

This chapter showed you the ins and outs of creating pitches, from subject line to description to product details. Before you move to the next chapter, here are a few final points to ponder:

- Proofread your work before you send out your pitch. A big typo in your subject line (e.g., "Dropboc unveils new iOS experience!") is the spinach-on-your-teeth of the blogging world.
- Less is more. Spend time trimming your pitches down to the basics. You want to excite and inform, but not overwhelm.
- Don't forget the video. It doesn't have to be polished or perfect; it just has to showcase your product.
- Motivate, motivate, motivate. Whether you are writing a pitch or your marketing text, your hook is your product's heart. Unless you explain *why* people should care, they won't.

Pitching Do's and Don'ts

There's art in pitching websites: skills you can learn, mistakes to avoid. Just as in any writing task, pitching involves time, thought, planning, and refinement. This chapter introduces basic do's and don'ts for you to consider as you prepare your marketing materials. There are subtle ways a pitch can go wrong, and important ways you can help strengthen your message. In this chapter, we write about a variety of how-to practicalities, from targeting to etiquette, to help you on your way.

As a developer, you probably don't want to get on the bad side of a blogger. Once you've made yourself unwelcome at the door of your favorite blog, it's hard to ever find open arms again. Even worse, you don't want to do that "special something" that takes you to a new level of notoriety among the blogging community. Word gets around on Twitter, on podcasts, and in personal discussions, and you don't want to be "that person."

What can you do to avoid the mistakes that could turn you into the wallflower at the App Store dance or the hardware soiree? In this chapter, we describe common mistakes that developers sometimes make when pitching products to bloggers and tell you how to avoid making similar gaffes. All it takes is a little knowledge about what others have done in the past to make sure that your pitch has a bright future.

Think of bloggers as your partners. They want to find exciting new products just as much as you want them to write about yours. Bloggers want to work with you to help promote good quality work. Even if you've created the best product that has ever existed, you may tick off bloggers by breaking basic rules of etiquette. Likewise, you may secure a great review just by being a good guy. Avoid alienating trends and position your pitch for the greatest possible effect.

Know the Site

Provide context when creating your pitch. The more you can explain your product, its niche, and its strengths, and tie it to a blog's interest, the better it will find traction and coverage. Not every blog is right for your product—and not every blogger is a good match for a review. A bit of groundwork helps you target pitches more effectively. Here are some handy ways to do that.

DO Address Requests to Specific Bloggers

When you know that a blogger has a prior interest in your product arena, leverage that knowledge. With regards to software, some bloggers specialize in tower defense apps, some in navigation apps, others in word puzzles, and others in Getting Things Done. Other technology bloggers focus on hardware and accessories (see Figure 4-1), with less of a personal and professional inter-est in the software side of the house. If you work in a field that crafts creative playthings, you might find some bloggers interested in fantasy cosplay, while others focus on SciFi memorabilia or manga. Authors might want to target specialists in romance, fantasy, political philosophy, or biographies.

Figure 4-1
Steven Sande is your guy for hardware reviews at TUAW.

Do a bit of research and direct your pitch to the person most likely to respond positively to it. Although most blogs provide a basic guide to their blogging staff, there's an easy way to find out exactly where the interest and expertise of each blogger is focused: Follow their writing over a period of time.

A personal pitch is appropriate, especially when you show that you've done your research. For example, "Dear Erica, I know you're really into German board games, and I have a product I am sure you're going to like." Refer to a previous review if you can tie your product into an ongoing coverage theme. "Dear Steve, I noticed you wrote a great review of Organize Lite, and I have a docking station that does something similar, but it brings a lot more—literally!—to the table…."

Connecting to people directly so long as it doesn't come across as creepy or stalker-like is both fine and encouraged. Just don't send the same pitch to multiple bloggers at the same site. When more than one reviewer picks up a personalized pitch, it causes lots of headaches, duplicated effort, and bad feelings.

Want an example of the "creepy, stalker-like" behavior we're referring to? Steve received a series of tweets from a developer pitching a new Mac app. Steve decided to see what the developer had to offer and responded to him. Now Steve's inundated with tweets asking why he hasn't yet written a review of the app. The answer? He wasn't impressed with the app, which duplicates a functionality that's already in Mac OS X. Now, he's also really not too happy with the overly enthusiastic developer.

DO Aim for Series Posts

The more you're familiar with a site, the better you can tie your pitch into the way the site does business. Site insight (forgive the aural redundancy there) helps promote product coverage, whether for a review, how-to post, or news post.

Slotting your product into a blog's columns gives your pitch an important context. It explains how the product fits into a site. For example, a typical series we work with at TUAW includes Product of the Day (e.g., iPhone App of the Day); on other sites, it might be T-Shirt of the Week or Cuddle Critter Du Jour, Holiday Gift Guide (see Figure 4-2), N Solutions for *Some Problem* (e.g., 10 Great iPad Keyboards for Travelers); or on another site, 5 Budget Moisturizers for Softer Skin), among others.

Holiday Gift Guide: 10 gifts for around 10 bucks

by Erica Sadun (Nov 15th, 2012)

It's a particularly tough time for families across the US right now, so we thought we'd try to find some budget-friendly alternatives for the holiday season. You can, of course, always make your own Apple-themed presents. Philipp Janssen's daughter helped decorate the corner of a MacBook Pro ...

Continue Reading

Figure 4-2
Most blogs feature regular columns that offer opportunities beyond basic reviews.

If you can aim your product at a series (like the TUAW Bookshelf, our DevJuice series for developers, etc.), you can smooth its way toward publication. Just make sure it's a good match and that you're not just reaching wildly for coverage. Series suggestions expand the way a blogger can consider your product, offering more write-up potential.

"I think this would make a terrific match to your *Budget Business Solutions* series," tells bloggers (1) that you are familiar with the site and (2) have thought about the best way your product might work on it.

DO Consider Being a Podcast Guest

Although most big blogs are primarily text and image oriented, don't forget that a lot of them have companion podcasts and video shows that are used to provide another media outlet. Offering to be on a podcast as a guest can be a good way to get word out about your product.

Podcasts can be either audio or video, and usually have a regular host or team of hosts. Spending 10 minutes or more explaining your app to the hosts and the podcast viewers/listeners can be effective in getting your story across. Podcast hosts are always looking for content for upcoming episodes, and are usually grateful when someone volunteers to talk to the audience about the product development process or perform a live demonstration. If there's a live chat going on at the same time, offer to take questions from chat room participants.

DO Consider Non-Review Posts

Bloggers will always consider suggestions of how your product works beyond a review. Expand your promotional possibilities by offering informed and smart suggestions on ways your product is ideal for coverage. Using site knowledge and articles you have seen onsite, pitch alternative takes on things using your product. For example, "I saw you discussed [product name] to do [some task or another]. We have a solution we think is better for the following reasons…." Bringing your product into the context of existing coverage offers a way for bloggers to continue telling an important story with fresh material.

Don't forget to pitch how-to and trend coverage with your product, not just reviews, for example, "Five ways to spring clean your hard drive" or "Interface trends bring a new freshness as designers move away from skeumorphism." This approach helps you in three distinct ways. First, it adds a new avenue for write-up. Second, your app is more likely to be written about in a non-critical/positive fashion. Third, the traffic on how-to posts often exceeds that on review posts. A write-up that says, "Here's a solution to solve some problem," typically receives more eyeballs than one on "Hands on with [Product Name]".

If you can tie your product into an ongoing news story, even better. When Spotify, the free streaming music app, first launched its service in the U.S., Erica installed it and found that its built-in sound controls weren't satisfying. After some investigation, she wrote up a post on how to use Rogue Amoeba's Audio Hijack Pro (see Figure 4-3) to independently adjust the treble and bass playback. The write-up got lots of page views and was a great promotion opportunity for Rogue Amoeba, whose CEO helpfully sent over a license code and assisted during post development.

A how-to that explains how consumers can use your product to solve a problem in the news (such as newly launched services, filing taxes, responding to hurricanes, political outreach, etc.) adds a useful hook for consideration. If there's one lesson here, it's that reviews aren't the be-all/end-all of any product's marketing strategy. All coverage is good when it gets your product out there into the public's eye in a positive way.

Figure 4-3
Your app can play a role in how-to posts, not just reviews. This post showed how to use Audio Hijack Pro to tweak Spotify's treble and base playback.

Scheduling Out

Bloggers love to plan ahead but only to a point. Our news-event horizon may extend out a week or two, but usually no further than that. On any given day, we hunt for fresh, newsworthy items. If your product isn't due to launch for three months, we probably won't be interested in doing a review yet. (We may, however, do a "coming soon" write-up, so don't think that you're completely out of luck.)

For early reviews, we're happiest working with short-term timelines of a week or two, especially when dealing with embargoed material. Under an embargo, posts go live when your product does. This early access gives bloggers extra time to test your product and allow it a more careful review than a last-second write-up.

Where you can, build time into your release schedule so bloggers can have that luxury of a slow review process.

DO Provide Specific Dates and Timelines

To make reviews happen, you must provide us with a specific set of dates and plans so we can schedule testing time, writing time, and work with embargoed releases. Try to avoid the "we just submitted this product for review" scenario, where your timeline is muddy or depends on a third party.

We can't count the times we bit on a review for a product we thought was pretty exciting and had the post sit waiting publication for weeks or months because of difficulties with getting that product to market. Remember this: Many bloggers don't get paid until their write-ups go live on the site.

It may sound a little selfish, but we'd rather you do the waiting before submitting the pitch than we do the waiting after we write an unpublishable item.

Steve cites a recent example where he was sent a hardware product in July that looked rather interesting and promising. He was about to write a review when he received a note from the manufacturer's PR firm asking him to hold off until August. Repeated delays kept the review from happening until December, when the PR firm basically told Steve to "go ahead and write a review, but note that we're not sure when the product is going to be available for sale." Needless to say, the manufacturing delays with this product were a topic of discussion in the review.

DO Bring Up the Topic of Exclusive First Looks

Bloggers love exclusives, especially when a first look comes earlier than your general release. First looks give websites extra prestige, and provide more publicity for your product. This works best, however, for prestige apps and hardware—not for another of a million tip applications, Tetris-style games, flashlights, or battery boosters.

If you have the clout, try to build a relationship with your favorite blog rather than changing the embargo rules for each product launch. It's understood that, sometimes, "Blog X" will always get the exclusives for a certain company—we'd like Blog X to be us, by the way—but don't jerk that expectation around too much. Either you create a universal embargo that applies across the entire blogosphere, or you build one or a few select relationships, which get early one-ups before the rest of the world.

Whatever you do, never offer an "exclusive" to more than one blog. It's a quick way to get yourself disliked and potentially banned. If an exclusive preview is offered to more than one blog, it's not an exclusive.

Definition of exclusive: Excluding or not admitting other things, restricted or limited to a single group or person.

DO NOT Jump the Gun

A developer contacted us this past autumn, offering an early look at an upcoming application. We had reviewed and loved some of his previous work, so we eagerly jumped at the opportunity. When Apple approved the application earlier than expected, he decided to release immediately. Over a weekend. After promising us an exclusive first look.

With Apple approving [app name] so quickly, it seemed important to launch the game asap. It appears the "New Releases" list sorts the titles not by their first availability date, but by their approval date!

Instead of leveraging an extensive exclusive overview, they received a modest general release and an undistinguished "app of the day" write-up later that week. It was a missed opportunity for both the developer and us, and one we remain a bit sad about.

Leverage Personality

We can't say this enough: There are real humans at the other end of that tip line. Be one yourself. Charm, warmth, and humor go far, especially for electronic communications. Let your personality sparkle as well as your product.

Just like you, this is our job. When we answer email, pick up the phone, or start IMing, we want to work with nice people. Kindness and courtesy are important social lubricants. We don't expect you to be a robot, and we're not either. The more you can engage with us on a human level of communications, the smoother things will run.

That's not saying there aren't drawbacks to creating that friendliness. Recently, we reviewed an application from an absolutely charming man, whose communication we enjoyed tremendously. Unfortunately, his utility wasn't up to snuff and we gave him a negative review.

All his notes cut off as if we'd turned the spigot, which was sad. We liked him and would have liked to continue the relationship to see what else he delivered in the future. A bad review doesn't mean we don't like you personally.

DO Offer Access

Provide access to your design team, company executives, and engineers. Reviewers like learning more about your app and the story behind it. Do not push these offers to the point of obnoxiousness. Sending monthly or weekly invites to talk with your CEO or be briefed by "industry experts" is simply not effective. Just include an option for contact in your pitch. "Have more questions? We'll be happy to set up a phone call with our CEO or dev team at your request."

DO NOT Hijack Conversations to Pitch Your App

Starting a fake conversation about a post you read "and loved" on the website, just so you can pitch your app in a roundabout manner, is bad manners. Pitch through the normal and appropriate channels. When you have a long-term relationship with a blogger, do feel free to give him or her a heads-up that you're about to do so. But, don't use that relationship to press for a review.

We can't tell you how many times after responding to an "Ask Aunt TUAW" question, the recipient responds with "Thanks for the info, by the way, let me pitch my app…." Don't do this. It feels sneaky, low, and unworthy. If a staffer writes back to you to answer a question, don't try to transform that into a stealth marketing opportunity. It doesn't work.

Hi Erica,

Great post on TUAW about the debacle with AT&T's $5/month data. I have always wondered why the cell phone companies are opposed to providing a data only plan for app developers.

Anyways, we developed an app that was recently accepted into the App Store called [Redacted]. We are looking for feedback from industry veterans such as yourself. I have provided the link to the app in the App Store. Would it be possible for you to provide us your feedback?

[Product info, and further pitch details]

DO Listen When the Blogger Offers Feedback

If a blogger sees your product as promising but with specific flaws, she may contact you and offer feedback. This is a courtesy and often done on her own time. If a blogger does so, please listen. You may not agree with the feedback that the blogger is taking personal time to offer you. You will not, however, manage to convince the blogger that he or she is wrong, no matter how much you argue.

Please don't argue, harass, yell at, or belittle bloggers. It seems pretty much common sense, but be as gracious as you can and take the feedback as you will. Some of it will be valuable, some of it will not. That's just reality. Bloggers are biased and opinionated. If we weren't, we wouldn't be blogging. A polite response goes a long way, especially with people you may work with again in the future.

A feedback call is simply a courtesy. It offers you more in-depth opinions than you might normally receive, especially if the blogger has declined a review. If you don't want this information, you can always say, "No, thank you." If the blogger is particularly obnoxious, you can cut short the call ("Have to run now! Thanks!"). Speaking as developers (as well as bloggers), your most critical users can be your most valuable, and bloggers approach products with an eye for criticism and evaluation.

DO Be Friendly

Bloggers are human, and they're usually friendly. A conversational tone goes a long way in establishing a relationship between you and the blogger. You don't have to be overly formal, but at the same time, you don't need to perform a comedy routine. Write using comfortable phrases, in your natural "voice," as if you were emailing a friend.

It's never wrong to say "Hi, Steve" or "Hey, Erica" in your email. You do not need to use titles like "Mr. Sande" or "Dr. Sadun" (or more commonly, and amusingly, "Mr. Sadun"). If we've met before, feel free to mention it in your correspondence, but then get on with your pitch.

Culture varies around the world. Most blogs operate with a relatively relaxed tone. Our most formal communications generally arrive from Asia. We often receive pre-pitch queries like this one. We respond by pointing to our tip line and invite a full pitch.

To briefly introduce myself, I am calling you from a mobile game publishing company called [Company] which is at Seoul, South Korea. We are greatly interested in promoting our company's mobile game in your review site.

We have variety of experience in publishing Android based games in Korean local market. However, we do not have experience in marketing iOS games in global. Since TUAW is globally known game review site, we would like to introduce our company game and arrange positive and beneficial articles regarding our games.

Anyhow, our company's mobile game is already launched in Korean local market and ranked first place. Our plan for [Company] is to launch at global iOS market by early December. We have already developed iOS version of [Product] and it is ready for its immediate launching.

I have included some screenshots and official trailer of our game, [Product]. If you like our game we'd love to know what the next step is for our game to be reviewed.

We look forward to a favorable response from TUAW. Thank you.

DO NOT Subscribe Us to Your Personal Email List

We're happy when developers consider us part of their success story. We're slightly less enthusiastic when they add us to their email blasts to family and friends about their latest successes. We love you, but please don't pepper us with enthusiastic updates about

Dear Friends, Family and those who took the time to help us, Because of you, your support, your guidance and your love, we are making our way into the world. Check out our latest article on [blog]. We are also on [blog]. [Name] and I are over the moon with all of this. Just wanted to share :)

Or

Keep getting the word out!!! We're gaining traction on the App Store, and you can help!

Or

Omigosh! We just got another post on [blog]!

Or

Awesome Job everyone! Looks like its starting to take off!

Instead, a simple thank-you will do, such as this:

Thank you so much for your write-up. It created an avalanche of coverage for us. After your post, we were covered on [blog], [blog], and [blog] – among others!

We delight in your success and are eager to hear about it. Just remember that a little good news goes a long way.

Communicate Well

If your pitch grabs a blogger's eye, but he or she doesn't quite understand the specifics, help clarify those questions by email or phone. Never assume that your press release is so perfect that it instantly conveys what your apps does and how it is positioned in the market. And never assume that the blogger covering your product has a background in your area.

Take it as a good sign that the blogger responded to you, and don't alienate that blogger by insisting on a full understanding of your market. Explain and repeat as needed. Allow bloggers to take the time needed to understand your product, and write about it semi-coherently.

There are several other ways you can best communicate about your product.

DO Leverage Success

This particularly applies in other markets (outside the U.S., for example) or on other platforms (like Android). If a blogger was not aware of your product, mentioning these related successes are great ways to strengthen your pitch.

Don't forget to namedrop your previous "winners," apps and products that were highly successful. If we can match a wildly popular product to you or some other positive history, it gives us much more interest in what you're going to do next.

DO NOT Name Drop Celebrities Unless You're Getting VC Funding

We are convinced that Apple co-founder and legendary nerd Steve Wozniak is a nice man. At the same time, we're well aware that he donates to many promising projects. Just because your Kickstarter got a Woz buy doesn't mean that he personally sanctions or promotes your endeavor. We get a lot of, "Have you guys seen this yet? Woz is a backer," emails. Not only do these mentions fail to give your product a boost, but they often work to your detriment.

The only time you should drop names is when a personality feels so invested with your company that they're providing significant venture capital funding, and are willing to issue statements on your behalf. Other than that, we tend to discount celebrity associations.

DO NOT Snitch on Competitors

They may have "snuck something through app review," but it doesn't reflect well on you when you play hall monitor to large tech blogs. Above all, take the high road and maintain your dignity.

DO Know Who You're Writing To

Never forget which blog you're pitching to and what material they actually cover. Little amuses bloggers more than receiving material that's misdirected or shows a basic lack of research and understanding about the site and its specialties.

- "Dear TUAW, you are a leader in Android screen cleaners…."
- "Dear MacObserver, I love you guys, you're way better than TUAW…."
- "We make the best Blackberry case EVER!"

Some of TUAW's most amusing app pitches begin "Dear Engadget," "Dear Ars Technica," and "Dear Leander." Addressing your pitch to the wrong website does not endear your product to bloggers.

Sites won't throw out the pitch, and they won't deliberately discount your application, but it starts you off on the wrong foot. If you can't be bothered to figure out which site you've pitched to, does your app's quality show the same lack of attention?

One of our favorites started, "We would really love to be reviewed on VentureBeat." It mentioned the developer had been personally reading and visiting that website for over two years. As a courtesy, we did forward the pitch to VentureBeat.

Be very, very careful with robopitches. "Dear `$website_name_primary`" (sic) and "I want to thank you for providing very interesting resource on `$opportunity_name_alt`!" (also, sic) aren't great ways to introduce yourself and the product you've invested so much time in.

Do your research. If you're pitching a website like TUAW, you probably don't want to send a pitch for "[*Technology*] Code Pal—Android [*Technology*] scanner, now available to download for FREE!" It's a waste of the blogger's time and of good electrons. Just because a site is on your full PR distribution list doesn't mean that every pitch from you is appropriate to send. Use good sense and avoid being added to smart email filters.

Of course, mis-sent emails aren't just limited to pitches. We get a lot of these, too:

Subject: Battery (Mac Book Pro)

What is your address and phone number in HCMC. I need a battery for my Mac Book Pro. Do you have (will be in on Thursday May 17th)? What is the cost?

Please no ads sent to my email--thanks.

Thanks, dick k.

> ### 🎙 NOTE
>
> Each website has its own submission policies. It's always appropriate to inquire politely how to submit your product for that site.

DO Avoid the "Ugly Sister" Scenario

Rolling along with a successful launch is a great idea, but never make a site feel like your second choice to the big school dance. Did you get a great review from iMore or from iLounge? That's great stuff, but it's not what you want to include in your pitch.

Telling a site that your app is promoted as New and Noteworthy with 5-star reviews in iTunes is great. Telling them that it was already hailed by big review sites like *fill-in-the-names-here* is pretty much counterproductive. Ditch the other site namedropping. No one wants to be a second thought.

What you mean to write is: "We got a great reception, we think you'll like our product, too." What we hear Is: "You're not important enough for us to have included you in our initial marketing roll-out."

It's sad, but true. A little judicial editing can give your pitch the celebratory spin you need without sounding like your target blog is a second thought.

DO Use Native Review

If you plan to deploy to the U.S. App Store, make sure you find native English speakers to review your pitch, application write-up, and details. If you don't have the right language skills, hire someone who does. Pass your application name and tag line through the approval of English speakers just in case what it sounds like isn't what you intended (*"In space, no one can hear you snatch"*).

When in doubt, be forthright about your language limitations. We'll be more likely to correct a few typos on your behalf when you give us a heads up, like this developer did:

Next wednesday I will launch a new iOS-game named [Product Name].

[Pitch details omitted here]

In case you need more information (or custom information/graphics), you could send me an email. Please note I'm not a native English speaker/writer, so there might be some grammar errors in the press announcement.

Greetings from The Netherlands,

[Developer name]

The same lessons go for English-speaking developers who plan to deploy globally. Always use native speakers to review and approve application elements. Major websites may not catch your non-English localization errors but your end-users will. As a rule, it's better to deploy English-only than to deploy bad localizations that may embarrass, offend, or anger native speakers.

Service bureaus like Traducto (traductoapp.com) offer press release, marketing material, and app translations, usually starting at about $0.10 a word.

You will see several examples of non-native reviews in Chapter 5, "Case Studies."

🎤 NOTE

One of our favorite websites, at least in terms of branding, is Urban Tool (https://www.urbantool.com/hq/), a German-run business. We are astonished that it decided to launch with that name—perhaps it didn't have a native speaker review—but the inclusion of a suggestive logo makes us smile (admittedly inappropriately) to this day.

Checking In

Reviews involve a delicate dance in communications. You want to promote your product and make sure you're not forgotten, but you don't want to harass the blogger in question. As a rule of thumb, it is *always* okay to check in with a blogger (once!) after they've requested a review unit or promo code, to ensure that they've gotten the material. This helps your product remain in the blogger's attention frame, and provides a good opportunity for you to offer support, team access, and so forth.

Excessive check-ins, on the other hand, are generally not a good thing. While it's okay to skip the back-and-forth reply order once, it's not something you want to make a habit of.

"Please, please, please don't send us three emails every hour asking if we've redeemed the promo code."

—Anonymous iOS Blogger

DO NOT Harass the Blogger

Here's a real-world letter (one, I'm afraid, of many):

Unfortunately I have not seen the review on your site, nor have I had any correspondence back from you regarding the game. Obviously I understand you are probably busy dealing with a backlog of emails/work. However if you could get back to me regarding the review status of the game, and whether or not you'd be interested in reviewing it - then I'd be very grateful.

If a blogger promises a specific (or close-to-specific like "next week") publication date, go ahead and ping them with something like: "Are we on target for next week? Anything else you need for your write-up?"

We know this product is your baby and you want to take good care of it, but we encourage you to balance your interests with patience and normal back-and-forth communications.

DO NOT Spam Bloggers

Avoid "floating your pitch to the top of the inbox." Here's an example from real life:

"Never heard back from you on this. I don't want us to lose an opportunity here."

And this, which "follow(ed) up" a non-existent conversation:

"Just wanted to follow up with you regarding some great apps for Father's Day."

And another:

"Just wanted to float the release of (Company)'s (App name) Free version to the top of your inbox. It's a fun, stealthy puzzle that game you can check out risk free."

This latter example was the fifth (!) ping about the app, none of which were responded to. If the blogger doesn't write back, he or she just isn't interested. Figure 4-4 shows the first three of those five unresponded pings.

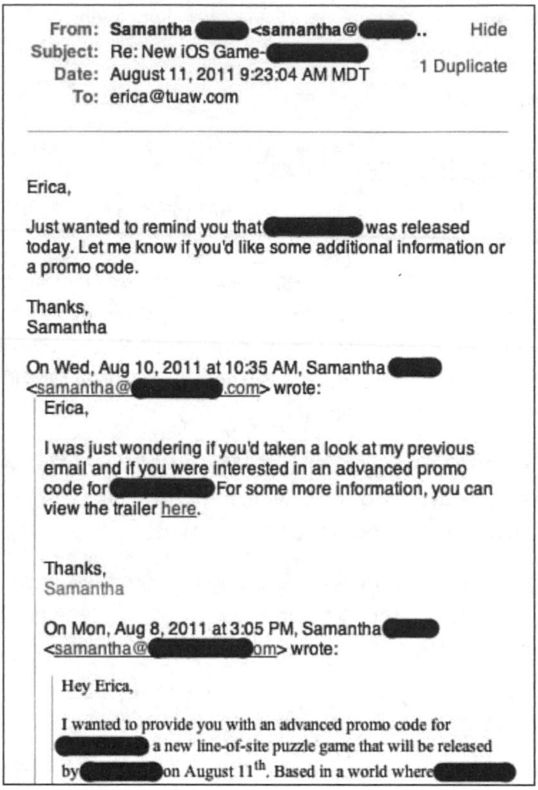

```
From:  Samantha ▓▓ <samantha@▓▓..        Hide
Subject:  Re: New iOS Game-▓▓▓
Date:  August 11, 2011 9:23:04 AM MDT    1 Duplicate
To:  erica@tuaw.com
```

Erica,

Just wanted to remind you that ▓▓▓▓ was released today. Let me know if you'd like some additional information or a promo code.

Thanks,
Samantha

On Wed, Aug 10, 2011 at 10:35 AM, Samantha ▓▓
<samantha@▓▓▓.com> wrote:

Erica,

I was just wondering if you'd taken a look at my previous email and if you were interested in an advanced promo code for ▓▓▓ For some more information, you can view the trailer here.

Thanks,
Samantha

On Mon, Aug 8, 2011 at 3:05 PM, Samantha ▓▓
<samantha@▓▓▓om> wrote:

Hey Erica,

I wanted to provide you with an advanced promo code for ▓▓▓ a new line-of-site puzzle game that will be released by ▓▓ on August 11th. Based in a world where ▓▓▓

Figure 4-4
Don't keep responding to yourself. It's not nice.

Figure 4-5 shows a typical response this kind of behavior may receive. Bloggers don't care if your client is paying you outrageous sums of money to promote an app. You become less and less effective over time if you employ these techniques—and it's a quick trick to the smart-filtering spam folder if you keep at this.

"Warning: [PRFlack Name] is RELENTLESS… if you get a review code, expect to be emailed regularly for the rest of your life. I tried [Product Name] and found the UI horrible, and decided not to review it, and I still get emails. Weekly."

—Unnamed Blogger

Thank you for your messages of the 23rd, the 22nd, the 22nd, the 20th, and the 16th, none of which I responded to.

I'm just sending you a courtesy letter to let you know that email is, in fact, working on my end, so you shouldn't worry that your emails aren't arriving.

Best regards,

Figure 4-5
Bloggers may respond to overly enthusiastic emails with snark.

NOTE

People rarely like things that float to the top of other things, whether they're dead fish, insects, or the contents of your commode.

DO NOT Presume That a Promo Code Request Leads to a Review

A promo code request gives bloggers a chance to look over an intangible good like a book or application. This allows them a closer look before making a call about whether the product makes a good fit to a review. After looking at the product, bloggers may decide to proceed with a write-up, or may (for a variety of reasons) move on to other products.

Passing on a review after requesting a promo code may occur for several reasons. Many bloggers avoid negative reviews except for big-name games where a buy/don't-buy scenario is valuable to their readers. In other circumstances, the product might be too similar to material already covered in recent columns or it may not "pop" in the reviewer's eye.

It is courteous for a blogger to tell you that the request involves "no promises." It's also kind to reply back when they've decided not to review the item after all.

DO Presume That a Tangible Product Request Leads to Coverage

The request-without-guarantees rule does not apply to hardware reviews. When you've sent a tangible product at a blogger's request, it's exceedingly rare that it does not receive coverage of some kind. Always follow up and check in, especially if the product is valuable and needs to be returned on a tight deadline.

Make sure that you provide return instructions and, where possible, return shipping labels. If the product can be turned over for a giveaway or donated to a local school, make that clear in your communications.

DO NOT Expect a Reply

It's harsh, but blogs generally do not respond to pitches unless the news is good and they have an interest in following up with you. Some developers submit their pitches to every major and minor possible review site they can find and never hear back from any of them.

If you do not receive any responses, it does not mean that your application is horrible but rather that no one bit on the hook. Your pitch may not receive a response for one of the following reasons:

- Your pitch may not have communicated effectively.
- The right person who reviews your sort of product may not have been around that day. Bloggers go to the doctor and take vacations.
- The product might have been redundant. ("But, we just covered that topic last week.")
- There are so many products, and so little time. Sad, but true.

DO Jump on Replies

If the blogger *does* reply to your pitch, *jump on it*! Our lives run on deadline, and if you take too long to get back to us, we may forget you. As TUAW blogger Kelly Guimont points out, "If you take three days to get back to me about the thing I want to…SQUIRREL!"

It's sad how many times we see a great pitch, reply back, and either never hear from that person again or receive an email weeks or months down the road. As a rule, don't send a pitch if you're not there to back up its marketing.

DO NOT Resubmit Your App Pitches

The human brain is finely tuned to detect redundancy. Resubmitting your pitch *will* get a blogger's attention, but not in a good way. A second, third, or fourth version of your pitch hurts your original without helping you at all.

The only exception to this rule is a highly personalized re-pitch that explains a motivating circumstance. For example, "I'm resubmitting this review request because I discovered that Mel was on vacation when I first sent it in and I know he's the go-to-guy for navigation app coverage," or "I originally sent my pitch in on the day Apple launched the new iPad. Please forgive me for sending it again. My original timing was awful, and I wanted to give my product a chance at a good start."

If your communication is human and personal, our response usually is as well. We are, by the way, completely over the "My dog ate my pitch" re-pitch joke.

Watching Your Timing

Nothing says "likely to be overlooked" than sending an email about your product on a big news day. We have received run-of-the-mill pitches on the day that a new version of OS X or iTunes was released, when updated iOS firmware debuted, when new iPhones hit the stores, and the day after Steve Jobs died.

If you check a website and see that all the coverage is about some big event, stop. Add a reminder note to yourself to try again in a few days or a week. But, don't pitch your app on a big red-letter news day. We will, like as not, miss your product in the excitement.

DO Accommodate Current Events

Consider postponing your launch should something unexpected and newsy happen to conflict with your initial push. In the Apple world, iTunes Connect allows you to reset your date of sale. Pull back and strategize as needed. It's better to give up a few days of sales than to be lost in the critical period when your product is just ready to go live.

Keep on top of the latest news and be sensitive to what's happening.

DO Build Opportunities

Although these events often work against you, they also provide opportunity to work for you. If you can figure out how to position your app within the current narrative, your app may have a huge boost, especially for existing products.

Does your app help solve some problem like keeping in touch during an earthquake or hurricane? Does it provide a photo gallery of someone recently lost? Does it connect to a popular movement that's gaining traction? Use current events to relate your apps to a potential audience.

Websites love being able to tie apps to the news. If you can figure out how your application does that, write it up and send it in. A topical connection can move your app straight to the top of the coverage list.

🎙 **NOTE**

Bloggers may get caught in a blast of news and forget to write a promised app review. The beginning of October 2011 was like that for a lot of us. Apple scheduled a major announcement for the iPhone 4S on October 4th, and then Steve Jobs died on October 5th. We were preparing for an upcoming iOS 5 release just a week later. When you don't hear from a blogger for a while, think about what's going on in the world. You may want to email a gentle reminder about finishing a review after that news settles down.

Gaming the System

Always represent yourself honestly when pitching to websites. Don't try to be cute and manipulate people. Here are some examples of ways some developers and publicists play things wrong.

DO NOT Astroturf

Your friends and acquaintances shouldn't be lobbying for reviews. It's not a grass roots movement; it's fake. It's quickly obvious when people try to astroturf sites, and it gains a lot of negative attention for you very quickly. Although Kickstarter projects tend to be the worst offenders, we've seen these kinds of hijinks for everything from software to accessories. Don't do it.

Subject: Found this new invention

http://www.kickstarter.com/projects/[redacted]

Found this little gem on kickstarter today and figured id pass it along to my favorite site! (love what you guys are doing). Anyways I did some research and couldn't believe that this tech isn't on the market already... I'm shocked actually. its worth a look I think.

Bloggers are also pretty good at smelling the 'turf at ecommerce sites. Is your product one that you "use all day at work!" or does it offer "much less hassle! Thanks!"? Is it a "smart idea!" or has a user been "using it all week and it hasn't failed me yet!" on the first day of release? Most of the time, astroturfed reviews are blindingly obvious in that they aren't written the way that people usually communicate and they're full of marketing aphorisms instead of honest feedback.

We notice and so will your customers.

DO NOT Offer to Pay for a Review or Prioritize Your Product

Reputable sites don't do that. Simply offering payment casts you as slimy in most bloggers' eyes.

Hi,

we are starting an iPhone/iPad application development business, and part of that we would like to get reviews of our apps on [website]. And all the possibilities on how can we be represented on your site. We need pricing on that.

Thank you for your time!

Best,

[Personal name]

And

Before going to the full process, we think that we should know about various features of "[Website]" for developers to promote their apps & the pricing strategy of [Website]'s different services.

And

We would like to ask if TUAW offer paid reviews. If yes, please let us know the rate.

Even worse is the developer who offers to "trade" favors, even if he does so in a friendly and amusing way:

I wanted to write you to see ask you to try our new game available in the App Store called, [Name!] Like every other app in that comes out, we would love a chance to be featured on your site. We are but a company of 1 designer, 1 developer and 1 PR person (who was not in charge of this letter). We don't have a whole lot to offer - we do have many things to trade. For example, I can:

A. Send you amazing pictures of unicorns everyday for 3 weeks.

B. GIve you Oprah winfrey's personal email address.

C. We can tweet regularly about the awesomeness of [Name]

D. I can send you and your staff a couple cans of slim jims I think they are worth a lot now that the macho man is no longer with us.

These are just a sampling of the things I can offer. If you have any other suggestions, please feel free to email me back at this email address and lets make this beautiful thing happen. Trust me, we would all love it. For real, we would love for you to help us get the word out in any way that you can!

It may be cute and funny on the surface, but the underlying message is off-putting.

DO NOT Try to Make Us Pity You

Pitch your strengths, not that you're "miserable" and "need to get noticed." Reviewers want to like you and care about your product, but you have to sell your pitch, not just evoke sympathy. We rarely care about the human-interest story motivating your product ("I wrote this for my daughter's birth" or "I wrote this in just 5 hours" or "I'm a high-schooler"). If you have a human-interest story, pitch that separately, not as a review request. Use a professional tone and talk about what makes your product stand out on its own.

When the App Store was new and fresh, and iOS developers were just beginning to tell us about their products, finding out that an app developed by a 14 year old had been accepted by Apple was big news. These days, we generally receive at least one or two pitches a week from some kid who has written an app and thinks this is newsworthy. Sadly, it no longer is. We want to judge an app on its merits, not the age of the developer.

DO NOT Pretend to "Just Be a Customer" and Talk About a Product You Just "Discovered"

If you really *are* a customer, that's a cool way to let sites know about overlooked products. It's the poseurs (and most of them are pretty obvious) that bother bloggers. Here's a real pitch that wasn't edited as carefully as the sender might have imagined. The emphasis is ours:

I am regular reader, and I very much enjoy when you mention great apps. I wanted to tip you about an app that Apple just featured on their AppStore. I was long time [Product] user but I was looking for alternatives due to the bad Mac support that [Product] offers. I found the app called [Product] **after Apple featured us**, and I've been moving data to it and using it actively for the last several days, and it's a masterpiece that one can rarely see in the AppStore. I think it will be good to write a review so other fellow-readers can learn about it as well.

DO NOT Quote Reviews Out of Context

Once you've gotten a review, don't play selective-quoting games, especially if you got an overwhelming negative review. Never quote the one positive comment and pretend that the rest of the review didn't happen.

As a serious developer, you don't want to hurt relations with websites when future products are at risk. Take the feedback seriously, and respond to it by improving your app. Bloggers aren't omniscient, and they aren't always right, but they do offer honest feedback that can help you identify where your app has strayed from where it could be better.

DO NOT Specify "Terms" for Your Review

The following is from a real pitch letter, which was sent along with a press release:

"Of course you may edit, add, or subtract from the provided information however I do require that you send me a final copy for approval before posting to your website."

You can imagine how well-received this letter was. Websites don't work this way. You cannot set the ground rules walking in.

DO NOT Lie and Mislead

During Summer 2012, we received a pitch for an adorable app. We loved it. However, it appeared to be based on a well-known cartoon. We contacted the developer and the rights holder about possible infringement. The developer wrote us back, saying he had clearance from the rights holder. He passed us the following quote, attributed to the brand manager:

"At this stage, I can see 'inspiration' but I can't see any infringement."

We went ahead and cleared the write-up and published it. Four days later, the rights holder got in contact with us, saying this was an out-of-context extract from a much longer email that requested a greater investigation into the matter and possible legal action.

Trying to deceive us is a great way to get a developer banned from our site. We will never cover this particular developer or his products again.

On a similar note, while we do care that you do have proper rights for materials you use in your application, you generally can skip legal disclaimers about the correctness or authenticity of baby names:

All the baby names are procured from various data sources and [COMPANY NAME] does not guarantee their correctness or authenticity and cannot be held responsible or liable for any issues or damages caused using this data.

We are still at a loss, wondering how inappropriate baby naming could cause damages.

Avoiding Offense

Every now and then, we deal with products that we believe to be offensive. We don't publish reviews for materials we find racist, sexist, or just plain repulsive. If your work lives along the boundaries of good taste, you may want to be careful when promoting it.

DO NOT Be Racist, Sexist, Etc.

We recently tested an app that had terrific gameplay. Its art and audio snippets, however, caused us to raise an alarm to management. The game, based on a German board game, included ethnic caricatures that pushed our comfort levels to the limit. After due consideration, a review was spiked, but we offered the developer another chance should he revisit the design in the future.

The developer explained that the brand was licensed, and he was not allowed to modify it. He failed to convince the rights holders to allow him to replace the national characters with professions or licensed SciFi characters. The game was not intended to create any political statement, but its potential firestorm kept us from covering it.

We passed on "My Booty Book" and the "Aroused Comrade Urban Camo aluminum case for iPhone." And, although the app was well intentioned, we also passed on "iBeg," which "simulates the life of a homeless person on the streets of Vancouver, BC." Some things just push our comfort levels beyond where we're willing to write.

Speaking of which, it's probably best not to put "big breasts" in your subject line when trying to get our attention.

DO NOT Burn Bridges

When you establish yourself at a website as a prolific (not to mention trollish) commenter, you may not want to submit your pitches under the same name and email address, lest the discussion you stir up is less about your product and more about your personal character.

Submitting Through Channels

Avoid submitting pitches to bloggers' personal websites and email addresses. Some developers do this as an end-run around normal app submission. It's not cool and it's inconsiderate.

Consider the following example, which combines two blogger pet peeves into one pitch. First, there's the once-reviewed person who hounds the blogger for another review. Second, it's a direct pitch, outside of blog channels. TUAW Blogger TJ Luoma explains, "Review hounding and direct pitching earns you my Gmail filter, which keeps your email from hitting my inbox, thus reducing the chance I'll ever see another email from you." Here's a request that arrived in his inbox from his personal website:

From: [Redacted]

Date: Fri, Mar 9, 2012 at 8:06 AM

Subject: Form Submission - Contact

To: [Redacted]

Message: Hi there,

I know this is probably not the preferred way to contact you about new apps. But I've been contacting tuaw through the official channel without any response. Since you liked my app [Redacted], I figure I might give it a shot.

[rest of the email snipped]

Just to add spice to the proceedings, TJ's website, the one that this pitch was submitted on, provides the following instructions in Very Large Letters. Regard:

Want to write to me about TUAW? Computers? Apple?

If you have a comment about something I wrote on TUAW please leave a comment there.

If you have an app that you would like to have reviewed on TUAW, submit it there instead.

If you are a PR person and would like to have your client interviewed for TUAW, contact pr at TUAW.com.

If you have a press release that you really want someone at TUAW to read, contact pr at TUAW.com

If your reason for contacting me falls under one of those categories and you've tried that already but didn't get a response and really really really think that you should contact me another way instead, please believe me, it's not going to make me happy to get a PR "pitch" through this form.

Luoma explains, "Contacting me through my web form, which specifically instructs you not to do that? Wow. I don't even know what the punishment for that is yet, but it's never ever going to end with me saying, 'Yes, you did everything I said not to do and now I'm going to reward that behavior.' Never. Gonna. Happen."

If wondering what the trifecta looks like, it's this. It's the unsolicited direct pitch that comes with a "Hey, just following up to see if you got my unsolicited email the other day." This Luoma promises will "earn you a custom Gmail filter, which skips the inbox, marks the email as read, deletes the email, and marks it as spam."

End Run Exceptions

So, when is it okay to make an end run around normal procedures and contact bloggers directly? Limit yourself to things that aren't pitches.

That is, if you're requesting a review, if you're sending a press release, if you're advertising, etc., go through channels. We probably don't want to hear that you're scheduling interviews with a company's CFO or receive invitations for a special briefing in our personal inbox, either.

We do, however, like to hear about really cool stuff. Are you doing something amazing and want to invite us into your beta? If you know us personally and already have a reasonably good guess that this is something that ticks our boxes, go ahead and send over a friendly human email about it.

If you don't already have that relationship established, send the same invitation through the blog feedback or comments form. We'll still receive it, and we are actual human beings at the other end of that contact form. You'll step on fewer toes by opening your lines of communication in that way. Typically, you can expect a personal response if someone has an interest and your conversation can continue from there.

We've met many extraordinary people building outstanding projects this way. We value those relationships and tend to keep the doors of communication open. Simply put, we want to see what else they'll build over time. Opening that initial door may seem a bit impersonal, but it helps prevent our personal lives from being overwhelmed by our professional email.

When to Pitch

Unless you are a huge company with a product that's been building buzz for weeks, months, or years (for example, Square Enix, Rovio, or Halfbrick on the app side of the house), most app developers will want to wait to submit pitches until they get Apple's green light. Once an app is approved, we encourage you to push that out in the iTunes Connect system so you have full control over your roll-out strategy. Hardware developers should usually wait until the product is shipping and can be purchased from real world vendors.

Knowing when your product is going live lets you slow down the marketing process and take control over how and when you wish to promote it. It gives you time to offer reviewers early access to a live product, especially in the case of the App Store. You can issue promo codes once the app has been fully processed and green lit even if you have not yet manually released it.

Offering one to several days' worth of advance warning is particularly valuable for any blog that schedules out software reviews. If you're looking to fill an "app of the day" slot on a site, offer scheduling flexibility so that the review appears with your app launch.

The 500-pound gorilla in this story is Apple. There are times we have written reviews for products that we simply cannot publish because Apple's review team never finished approving the app. One of our recent Mac Daily Apps (DragonDrop; https://itunes.apple.com/us/app/dragondrop/id499148234?mt=12) took months before we could write about it.

When Apple finally got around to rejecting it, we wrote it up as an independently distributed app and helped create a grass-roots movement to convince Apple to reconsider. They did, and the app is now available for sale in the Mac App Store. We reviewed early because we felt passionately about its utility, but our review remained in stasis as we waited on its approval.

If possible, avoid submitting your product until you know that it's sellable. Yes, we're always interested in early access for products that are *amazing*, but few products meet that threshold.

Dealing with Apple Review Headaches

Despite the delays, frustrations, and other headaches involved with Apple's store review process, there are good (monetary) reasons to aim your product at its store. When you're an app developer, lots of possible venues compete for your attention, including the App Store, Amazon, and the Android Market. Which one is worth your time and energy? We turned to Avatron Founder and CEO Dave Howell for the answer. Here's what he had to say, in a topic we first discussed on TUAW (http://www.tuaw.com/2012/05/08/devjuice-should-i-develop-cross-platform/).

Avatron makes Air Display (see Figure 4-6), a popular app that allows you to use a mobile device like an iPad or phone as an extra display for your computer. When you're on the road, it's nice to be able to offload a Twitter stream, for example, onto a secondary screen so your laptop can be dedicated more to your work.

Figure 4-6
Air Display offers a handy way to connect a mobile device to your computer for use as an extra screen.

Air Display is now available across a number of platforms, including the following stores: Apple iOS App Store (iOS), Apple Mac App Store (Mac), Google Android Market (Android), Amazon Appstore (Android), Samsung Apps (Bada), and Intel AppUp (Windows netbooks).

Given the time investment, the overhead, and general work involved in developing cross platform, where has Avatron seen its strongest sales? You won't be surprised by the answer: in the iOS App Store. Like many other developers, Avatron found that the App Store delivers customers and product interest in ways that other platforms have been unable to match. Howell lays out Avatron's AirDisplay sales as follows:

- iOS App Store: Strong sales
- Mac App Store: 1/10 of the sales of the iOS App Store
- Android Market: 1/2 of the Mac App Store sales
- Samsung Apps: 1/5 of Android Market
- Amazon App Store: 1/10 of Android Market
- Intel AppUp: "4 copies in over an entire year," and Howell bought one of those copies.

In other words, for every 1,000 sales for iOS, Avatron roughly sees 100 in the Mac App Store, 50 in the Android Market, 10 on Samsung, and 5 on Amazon. The numbers speak for themselves.

Each store has its strengths, weaknesses, and quirks, but Howell is clear about one thing: No matter how App Store developers complain, "iOS is the most painless of the bunch. And this is coming from a developer whose latest iOS app was pulled by Apple without any credible justification."

Avatron retired Air Dictate, the app pulled from the App Store by Apple, in January 2012. "Our most recent submission of Air Dictate did not break any rules, or use any private APIs," Howell said, discussing the background of that situation. "Apple pulled it because it bizarrely claimed that apps that 'relate to Siri' are infringing Apple's Siri trademark or copyright. I sent them the email addresses to three Apple IP lawyers so the app review team could get a tutorial on what exactly trademarks and copyrights are, but my helpful suggestion have proved fruitless so far."

Compared to other stores, however, Apple's App Store offers the simplest road to market and the best logistics. "The latest move by Google requires Android Market sales to go through Google Wallet. No more PayPal, Zong, or Boku. And now, Android Market is called Google Play," Howell explained. "I can't keep up with the thrashing. And Google still offers no way to give out promo codes, or even to purchase a copy of an app for somebody else. Apple's way, way ahead in this kind of logistics."

Howell pointed out that Amazon remains U.S.-only. "Amazon does let us buy gift cards for people, which is nice. As long as they're in the U.S. and they don't mind getting their apps through Amazon Appstore. Amazon's review process is no faster than Apple's, and strangely, it's much slower to get an app approved for Amazon's own Kindle Fire than for other devices. So, their own customers get our apps later than everybody else."

Wrapping Up

Fortunately for developers and manufacturers hoping to get the attention of bloggers, there are some relatively easy rules to follow that make it easy to write a pitch that works. Some of the key points in this chapter include the following:

- Take the time to get to know your target websites. Become familiar with the focus of the blog, the people who write for the blog, and any special feature series that might be useful in introducing your product to the world.

- Be friendly in all of your dealings with bloggers, as a little courtesy can go a long way toward establishing a long-lasting relationship. Remember, bloggers are people, too!

- Once you've sent in your pitch, follow up, but don't be obnoxious about it. Most bloggers are extremely busy and can't always immediately respond to all of your emails.

- Don't game the system. Nothing infuriates a blogger more than someone who uses underhanded methods to try to obtain coverage of a product.

5

Case Studies

Good pitches excite, intrigue, and engage. At best, bad pitches may provide amusement to a blogger. The examples in this chapter highlight both successful pitches and ones that could use improvement. You'll see what works in each of these pitches and what needs a bit of attention as we share real-world examples of pitches from our inbox.

We tried to cover a variety of instructive situations in this chapter. We've obviously added a few cases to share some smiles, but we're hoping these examples also convey deeper lessons.

Each of these case studies represents a real pitch for a real product in a real situation. Businesses depend on these pitches. There are developers who have spent considerable time creating the products they're writing to us about. You may be surprised that we were, in fact, interested in some of the less perfect examples that crossed our desk.

We responded to machine-translated awkwardness, we've bit on pitches that left out critical pitch elements, and passed on pitches that were extremely well written. We included this chapter to provide a real-life grounding to contrast with the do's and don'ts covered in the previous chapter.

In the end, form matters, but only so much as it helps convey your message. We're always far more interested in the product you're trying to communicate about than how you put it in your email. All those tips and tricks we cover throughout this book should help you become more effective at sending that message. Ultimately, your product and its capabilities is what we're looking for.

Case Study: Short But Sweet

The following is an excellent pitch from Lucidus Apps for its Translator+ Mac App (see Figure 5-1). It doesn't include all of our recommended elements, but it sells itself without any excess work. It leverages a brief, memorable description to communicate just enough details to get the job done.

Figure 5-1
Translator+.

Subject: Please review our Translator+ Mac App.

Here is the Mac App Store promo code for you: XXXXXXXXXXXX

(App Store page: http://itunes.apple.com/us/app/productname/ id445180990?mt=12)

Translator+ is the simplest translation tool to help you get a word or paragraph translation instantly. Powered by Microsoft® Translator, it supports 34 languages and gives you accurate translation.

Select. Translate. It's that simple.

There's really not much more needed here to grab a blogger's attention, although the subject line could be more descriptive. The pitch provides a promo code and a link to the App Store page. The summary is precise, and the final catch phrase sums up the product for sale.

Well done indeed.

Case Study: The Solid Query

Despite a few issues with proofreading, the following example from Softsign (see Figure 5-2) shows a good, solid query. The app description is particularly strong. Once read, you know exactly why the product is valuable and where it fits into a usage niche. It also provides a human voice, highlighting the person behind the development.

Figure 5-2
Softsign for iOS allows users to sign PDFs with their fingers.

I wanted to let you know about an App we have developed in case you were interested in writing a review?

Softsign is an App which allows users to sign PDF documents and JPEGs on screen (with your finger or a stylus) and then email them directly from the App - eliminating the need to print, sign and scan documents. It's legally binding and we are seeing strong traction from the SME community here and in the US and Europe (35,000 users after two months).

You can download the App for free here: http://itunes.apple.com/gb/app/appname/idxxxxxxxxx?mt=8&ls

If you need any more information please don't hesitate to contact me. If it's not of interest then thank you for your time.

I look forward to hearing from you.

Not only was this a successful pitch, we really liked the app upon reviewing it.

Case Study: The Professional Pitch

There's a reason people hire PR firms. They do marketing every day, providing both introductory pitches and full press releases. Consider the following material prepared for an iOS game called Smoody (see Figure 5-3) by Chi Zhao when she worked at Appular PR.

This email introduces a major application update and short-term sale, a great combination for getting bloggers to take a look after a successful initial launch. Zhao has included all the information needed to describe the app ("colorfully animated physics-based iOS game") and to explain what's new (via bulleted points). To support this message, she included an assets attachment, links to a video, pricing details, and so forth.

The announcement is sparse and to the point, without wasted effort. This is the kind of communication you should try to mimic.

Figure 5-3
Smoody's update caught our eyes.

Smoody Updates with new Levels

With over one million downloads in a single week following launch, Smoody became an instant hit on the iOS platform, and was the #1 top downloaded app in the US App Store.

Today, Smoody announces the release an update for their colorfully animated physics-based iOS game! It now includes five different environments with over 100 mind-bending levels!

Update Includes:

- 20 new levels in an underwater chapter, The Ocean

- Five new characters to discover

- Game Center and OpenFeint leaderboards and achievements

- Facebook and Twitter integration

I have included a copy of our press release along with video and image assets below. Feel free to let me know if you're interested in reviewing this app! :) Watch the Trailer: http://www.youtube.com/watch?v=zjFm3SQw0ok

To celebrate this launch, Smoody and Smoody HD will be available for FREE on the iTunes App Store:

Smoody for iPhone and iPod touch: http://itunes.apple.com/us/app/smoody/id421953010?mt=8#

Smoody HD for iPad: http://itunes.apple.com/us/app/smoody-hd/id429274014?mt=8

Normally, they're available for $0.99 and $2.99, respectively.

Best, Chi

Case Study: The Lost Holiday Opportunity

The app developer in the following letter does one thing exactly right. He tied his product release to an upcoming holiday, allowing him to leverage blog coverage. Blogs love covering holiday apps for New Year's Day (resolutions, health and weight loss), Valentine's Day (dating apps and apps for couples), St. Patrick's Day (beer apps), Shrove Tuesday (pancake apps), and so forth throughout the year. If you can tie your app to a holiday, it's an excellent way to pitch it to websites.

Hello,

I am the developer of a [topic] app for the iPhone, iPod Touch, and iPad. The app is called [product name] and I was wondering If you could mention it on your website for [upcoming holiday]. I would greatly appreciate if my app could be mentioned on this awesome site.

Thank You very much!

[Developer name]

What this developer fails to do here is motivate his application in any other way. He doesn't explain how his app works in the context of the holiday or provide any of the basic links and descriptions that would sell the concept further. What's missing is "This is the perfect app for this holiday because...." Go beyond the holiday name into a direct tie to its celebration.

Never assume that your reader will immediately "get it." It's worth taking the time to explain and motivate, even if your app is a Jack-o-Lantern for Halloween. Take a few lines to explain how your app works within the holiday context and how it stands out from the crowd. This is a real lost opportunity, because he offers the right kind of app at the right time of year, but without a few supporting lines of information that would help promote it effectively.

Don't forget the extra work involved here for the blogger. There are no URLs to any product page whatsoever. The blogger will need to start tracking down the app manually to see if it will be a good match to the holiday coverage.

Case Study: The Meh Pitch

Your application write-up should *pop*. It should excite potential reviewers just as much as it excites you. After all, you just spent however long sweating over its development. Here's an example of a pitch that just didn't engage us.

Our company just released a new iPhone game called [Product Name] which is available for free on AppStore. This is very simple time killer but it features unique and very charming creature [as named].

When the game begins the player places their finger over [product feature] and waits until [an event occurs] at which point the player should react quickly by [responding to that event].

We would like to ask you if you could do a review of the game on your web site.

The problem with this pitch lies in how dull the application sounds. It's a game app, but it doesn't inspire fun. Where's the excitement? Where's the hook? Contrast that pitch with how it could have been. Here's how we envision trying to sell the exact same app, but with a little pizzazz.

Watch your fingers! You don't want to lose them to [the charming creature]!

[Product name] introduces a fun and exciting assessment of your reaction time. Think you can best [the charming creature]? Put your skills to the test with this free app, now available from the iTunes App Store.

Yes, our rewrite isn't ideal, but it introduces the notion of challenge and excitement that's distinctly lacking in the original. This revised pitch uses its introduction to grab attention and follows it up with a motivational statement that explains why the app stands out.

Always ask yourself, "What is my app's big idea?" Use that idea to help your app stand out and intrigue the reader.

Case Study: The Completely Inappropriate Pitch That Made Us Smile

Sometimes, a mismatched pitch can still win a blogger's heart. The following software was in no way an appropriate match for the website, yet we were utterly charmed by the letter. Its English is awful but at the same time, the pitch *pops*. You know exactly what this application offers and who its audience is. The author's enthusiasm projects past any language barriers (or issues of squickiness). No matter what you think about apps of this nature, the gusto shines through.

Dear Sir and Madam

I'm writing for request a review of our photobook app. We are delivering many apps in Japan. We would like to expand our market in USA as well. We have already delivered some apps in USA app store. I'm requesting the app review to your website.

Here is [name]; Japanese hot gravure babe photobook. She is known as a gravure idol in Japan. Her attract point is a big breast. It is going to come out from her bikini..... She is in a island in this photobook and playing around at the beach. She also exploring in the forest. You can feel you are travelling in the island with her. Enjoy her sexy posings and smiles.

Downloading and browsing bikini photos by iPhones and iPods are available. Downloaded 100 fabulous photos.

It is not allowed under 17 years old to download this pics.

Definately don't make you regret to purchase this photobook. Don't miss it!

3. iPhone app link; http://itunes.apple.com/us/app/idxxxxxxxx?mt=8

I hope you would put this apps to your website. Please do not hesitate to contact me at any time.

Sincerely, [developer name]

To this day, "attract point" has become our insider meme for don't-miss application features.

Case Study: Winning by Charm

Some pitches win us over with simple charm. That said, we have about as much interest in cord detanglers (see Figure 5-4) as we do in sheep intestines. But, how can anyone ignore a pitch as clever and on the mark as this one? We loved it.

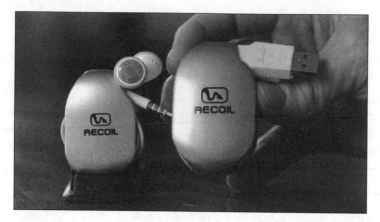

Figure 5-4
The Recoil Cord Winder.

Dear TUAW,

There are moments in history when a particular person in a particular place has the chance to re-direct the course of humanity.

In 460 BC Hippocrates launches the age of Modern Medicine.

In the 1600's Papin perfects the Steam Engine

In 1928 Alexander Fleming invents penicillin.

In 1976 Bill Gates ushers in the era of Modern Computers

In 1965 James Brown invents Funk.

Now, in 2012, TUAW has the opportunity to impact humanity on a near similar scale. Through the power of TUAW's epic influence over the clicking pattern of it's readers, TUAW alone can save humanity from the inevitable collapse of modern society due to the overwhelming accumulation of tangled cords and cables which is at the root of so much human despair.

Cordpocalypse!

By following this link: http://kck.st/xZHQRk, and exposing your readers to the revolution-ary technology contained therein, the name TUAW is likely to be included in the history of human achievement reserved for only the true visionaries.

Thank you for your courage, and your focused determination to put the future of our species above whatever current editorial schedule you might already have in place.

Humbly in your debt,

David Alden

David's pitch was smart, funny, and it sells his product (in this case, a Kickstarter project) far better than "please look at my cord detangling solution." To be honest, we did end up passing on this project, but it wasn't because his pitch failed; it was due to the product itself. There's only so much enthusiasm for cord technology we can muster, no matter how brilliant the pitch.

Case Study: Completely Missing the Mark

Sometimes, a pitch just gets it wrong, all wrong. From the topic of the pitch ("Android applications") to the auto-translated language used within, this pitch reflects a low level of detail oversight:

We development android applications "NIPPON MELODY MAKER"

Nice to meet you. My name is K. M. We have been producing music and video and application development in Japan. This time, I made a music distribution application. A lot of Japanese anime theme song. It revives all types of music from latest to old favorite of Japanese anime theme songs. It is one of the free downloadable music synthesis application of media player and the music store. All the purchasable music of our store are high quality.

Please check my URL (Not included) Thank you Kind regards

That's not to say that poorly targeted pitches are limited to foreign requests. Here's one that didn't understand that TUAW doesn't review Android products:

I am co-founder of [redacted]. We have recently published our first game called [redacted]! We are launching it for Android here in the next week or so, and I was wondering if you guys would check it out for an App-a-day review or something! We would be more than happy to send a few promo codes your way! Please let me know if this is not the proper channel for this, as we are just getting off the ground, but would love to share this addictive retro-style game with you!

Thank you for your time!

Make every pitch count. Consider who you are sending the pitch to and why it's a good match to their website.

Case Study: The Perils of Autocorrect

Here's a pitch that introduces a "fermium model solution." What's the app doing with that synthetic element (see Figure 5-5)? The developer probably meant "freemium," the business model where apps are offered for free with premium purchases leveraged after that initial sale. The lesson here is this: Beware of autocorrect!

We have created a really cool new app that is a fermium model solution. For free users can add documents that they want to keep with them on their iPad or iPhone. For $.99 they can use the app as a better FAVORITES button for their DropBox or Google Docs documents. And for $20 a year--they can keep documents in-sync with other devices, share easily with users and upload stuff online...

Autocorrect is *not* your friend, although we think the atom would work pretty well as a low-end (perhaps overly busy) icon.

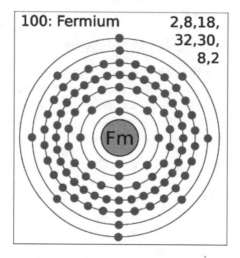

Figure 5-5
Fermium is a synthetic element. Its symbol is Fm and its atomic number is 100.

Case Study: Buzzwords

Some pitches are so full of buzzwords that we have to work too hard to figure out what the developer is getting at. Write simply. When in doubt, put your pitch through a "reading level" calculator. There are dozens available via a simple Google search.

Common readability metrics include the Gunning Fog index, Flesh Kincaid Grade Level, Automated Readability Index, Coleman Liau index, and the SMOG readability index.

You can easily find automated tools (http://www.online-utility.org/english/readability_test_and_improve.jsp) to grade your writing. Paste in your pitch and see exactly how hard your text is to understand on its first reading. For example, consider this pitch:

[Redacted] is a dedicated browser that lets you preview, edit and screenshot your responsive site at any size from mobile through to large desktop. Focus your responsive workflow with a tool that doesn't rely on bookmarklets, restrictive pre-defined breakpoints - or even a web connection. [It] improves on web-based tools by letting you create and work on multiple breakpoints simultaneously, even setting custom user agents if required. [It] also allows you to preview and debug fluid variations inside your media queries with our unique "Range" functionality - all without having to resize your browser ever again. [It] allows you to capture full viewport screenshots of all open breakpoints for sending to clients, supporting blog posts or assessing layout. Of course [it] doesn't require a web connection so you can work uninterrupted when traveling or when a connection isn't available.

Or this one:

With the pressure to validate an increasingly complex set of testing requirements across different applications architectures and interfaces, multiple mobile OSs, form factors, and network technology layers, [we] forecast cloud and mobility applications will help propel worldwide testing services to an impressive 15.4 percent annual growth rate through 2015.

Would love to wire you into this announcement and discuss this new cloud sync functionality to enable greater collaboration and synchronization with ease between developers and all project stakeholders.

If a pitch requires a graduate level of education to read comfortably, you probably want to re-write it to make it simpler, friendlier, and more comprehensible.

Aim for a reading difficulty below 8th grade. You won't insult the bloggers; you won't insult the customers reading your marketing text. Detangle your writing and your audience won't have to process complicated sentences.

Figure 5-6 shows the score for the above pitch snippet. The webpage used to calculate these numbers states, "The measure of readability used here is the indication of number of years of education that a person needs to be able to understand the text easily on the first reading."

Number of characters (without spaces) :	734.00
Number of words :	139.00
Number of sentences :	6.00
Average number of characters per word :	5.28
Average number of syllables per word :	1.74
Average number of words per sentence:	23.17
Indication of the number of years of formal education that a person requires in order to easily understand the text on the first reading Gunning Fog index :	13.58
Approximate representation of the U.S. grade level needed to comprehend the text : Coleman Liau index :	14.01
Flesch Kincaid Grade level :	13.99
ARI (Automated Readability Index) :	15.02
SMOG :	13.49
Flesch Reading Ease :	36.03

Figure 5-6
Simplify your writing. Readability indicators can help you judge how you're doing.

Case Study: Not Enough Detail

Sometimes, simplicity isn't enough. Although the intent is worthy, the developer fails to offer enough information to make us want to use that promo code he sent along.

Subject: our new app

We've released a new app and would love if you review or comment on it.

Here's a promo code: N3Y6739AJN43

Here's another one, which at least mentions the name of the product and its category.

Hi,

could you please review my memory game, [Product Name]?

Thank you

And another, which offers us, well, nothing.

Subject: I need a review

I have app to submit

In many cases, less is more, but don't take it to the extreme. Always give bloggers something to go on. Unless you provide that structure to explain your app, your pitch is heading straight to Mail's trashcan.

Case Study: The WTF We Don't Even Pitch

Death can be set only when all the timer is not running.

[Redacted] is a simple app that only four timer. Kitchen timer, photo film developing, learning presentation, please use to demonstrate the speed of imagination, such as eating contest hot dog.

You can set the "second" and "minutes" in the screen for each timer. Four timers will operate separately. It is also possible to operate four successive timer. Continuous mode switching, please click the Settings icon. Death can be set only when all the timer is not running. Sound when the time is up.

1. Bell 2. Harp 3. Game Clear 4. Bow 5. Vibe (no sound)

We know. Us, too.

Case Study: The Pitch That Got Away

We received the following pitch in Autumn 2012 and replied, hoping to take a look at the product. And then, we never heard back from the developer. Yes, the pitch sounded a bit odd with its uppercase APP mentions and stilted tones, but it sounded like one that might be of interest to a segment of our readers.

Dear Sir or Madam:

I have recently created my first "APP". I would be extremely grateful if you would review my APP. This would be invaluable to its success.

The APP is called OCD, which stands for Obsessive Compulsive Disorder. This is something that I have researched in great detail both as a Radiographer and Nurse, and as a previous sufferer. It is estimated that a significant proportion of people will suffer with OCD. It is also a factor in many disorders and social issues, as my research will demonstrate.

My APP contains a clear and concise description of OCD, has a test to ascertain the level of OCD being suffered, and includes treatment options. The APP provides Cognitive Behavioral Therapy, the leading treatment for OCD, among other issues.

My app is considerably cheaper that its competitors.

Please consider my APP for your publication.

Cognitive Behavioral Therapy (CBT) is an area in which several bloggers on our team have a background and interest. We regularly cover topics about assistive technologies and creative uses of Apple technology for age and physical challenges. Although the phrasing is odd, and the author may or may not be a "previous sufferer," it's a topic that caught our interest and one that we wanted to pursue but couldn't.

Case Study: Don't Submit Multiple Products All at Once

This is not a hard and fast rule actually, because we do respond to multiple product requests most typically from hardware developers. It's common for them to suggest that they send us a group of items to test. However, we do not treat product submissions as "tickets." We don't open a review queue to investigate each request. Therefore, you're generally best off individually submitting each app you'd like us to review.

Of course, it's also best to describe and name the apps in question in your pitch. Sadly, the developer who sent along the following pitch did not:

I would like to submit these 3 iOS app reviews to tuaw.com:

http://itunes.apple.com/us/app/….

http://Itunes.apple.com/us/app/….

http://itunes.apple.com/us/app/….

Thank you

Related URL: http://

Case Study: Machine Translation

Imagine trying to sell your application in a foreign country, one whose language you do not speak. TUAW blogger TJ Luoma asked us to include this tale of a young Italian app making its way in a far-away land via a machine-translated pitch that was *just* coherent enough to catch our interest.

Hello, I'm writing to announce my new application with which you can not miss the most: Has it ever happened that the phone will ask where you are and you do not know the way? Or do you need to know the zip code of the area and you should always ask someone? with this, you can see exactly who you [URL redacted]

The pitch, as hard to understand as it was, did sound interesting. So, TJ clicked the App Store URL to get more information about the app. What did he find? An app description in the U.S. App Store written entirely in Italian, as shown in Figure 5-7.

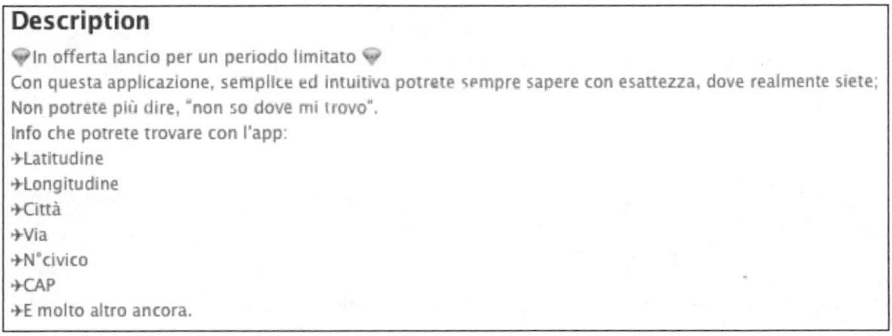

Description

♦In offerta lancio per un periodo limitato ♦
Con questa applicazione, semplice ed intuitiva potrete sempre sapere con esattezza, dove realmente siete; Non potrete più dire, "non so dove mi trovo".
Info che potrete trovare con l'app:
→Latitudine
→Longitudine
→Città
→Via
→N°civico
→CAP
→E molto altro ancora.

Figure 5-7
Non si parla italiano.

As many independent developers are popping up all over the world, this type of pitch and product description situation is becoming more common than you might first imagine.

Whenever possible, especially when requesting reviews from major American blogs, hire a native speaker (Google Translate doesn't count) to produce English-language marketing materials for your App Store entries and, hopefully, your pitch letters.

We think that this is an app we'd have been interested in. Unfortunately, the communication barrier proved insurmountable.

TJ notes, "Make sure your app description page is in a language that can be read by the people you want to review it. If you hope to reach a wide audience, make sure it's available in English -- the de facto lingua franca of the Internet."

Case Study: Avoid Unspecific Bullets

Bullet points push key features that should catch bloggers' and purchasers' eyes. They are a major structural element for many pitches, letting you offer tasty selling points with minimal words. You see them so often because they work so well. A well-designed bullet list condenses reasons people should buy a product into a single visual stack.

When added to your pitch, make sure they present information that differentiates your product, not just describes it. Each bullet point should pop with a great sales idea. Here's an example where a pitch went wrong with its bullets.

Hey Blogger,

I have a product you might be interested in checking out - It's a really cool and practical program that helps people keep and plan their trips in a better way, and has the following hot features

1, Ease of using.

2, User friendly and clean interface.

3, The first kind of truly travel route planner......

You can get some more information from our product site.

And if you think you might be interested, drop me a note and I'll forward you something. Thanks for taking time to read this mail. I look forward to hearing back from you.

Regards,

Sadly, none of these bullets stands out to sell the product. Worse, point 2 merely restates point 1, and neither explains *how* the product offers a unique user experience that sets it apart from the field. Plus, we can assure you that we've seen lots of "truly travel route planners" in our time.

When you include lists in your pitches, make sure each point motivates and sells your "hot features." For example, the developer here might have pushed "an amazing user-centric design," maybe one that "limits the number of touches used to select a route," or "a planner that adapts to your user's itinerary, not just his destination." There are lots of ways each point could have been expanded and explained.

Case Study: The Excellent Response

We often reply to pitches with queries when we don't quite get how the product fits into its competitive field. For example, we received a pitch from Charles Teel about his ActivePrint app. He wrote, "After a great deal of input from Mac users, we have just released a beta version of our popular ActivePrint app for the Mac OSX platform." Erica responded, asking, "We've covered quite a lot of these in the past—how does your app move past Printopia features to offer something compellingly new?"

This is where Charles did an amazing job. Unlike many other developers who respond to these kind of queries by repeating the same information from the original pitch, he wrote back with a thoughtful and incisive description differentiating his product from the competition.

Excellent question! When compared to Printopia I would say that ActivePrint's unique feature is range. Basically Printopia will make any printer an AirPrint printer. However, the limitation of AirPrint printers is that your iPad or iPhone has to be on the same WiFi network as the AirPrint printer. As a result, this is tethering you to your home network if you want to print. To me, that kind of defeats the purpose of being mobile with these kinds of devices.

With ActivePrint, you get the advantage of our Cloud Printing service. This allows you to not only print to your PC's printer while you're geographically near it, but also while you're across town or across the world. All you need is an internet connection for your iPad or iPhone. As an example you could do work at home on your iPad, and have the document printed on your office printer across town. Or if you're on vacation and you take photos with your iPhone, you can send those photos to your printer back home right after you take the photos. In both scenarios, you're not having to wait until you're near your printer to print your content. Instead, your content is waiting for you in your printer tray by the time you get to your office the next day or back home after your vacation.

With AirPrint solutions like Printopia, you have to wait until you get home from vacation and then go through the process of deciding which photos you want to print. Or in the work from home scenario, wait until you get to the office and try and remember which documents you needed printed. After you've done, then you have to wait for the printing to complete. While you're going through all of this, you could have already had it all waiting for you in your printer tray when you showed up if you had ActivePrint.

His correspondence explained the way his product fit into the market and showcased its abilities and potential.

He got his review.

Case Study: The Pitch Rewrite

Although most pitches aren't awful, many can be improved upon with a little work. Brian Atz of Essential App Marketing is a tremendously good sport. He allowed us to take one of his real-world pitches for iDashboard (http://www.idashboardapp.com/), break it down, and suggest improvements for the purpose of this book (see Figure 5-8).

Figure 5-8
iDashboard for iOS.

The Original Pitch

Here is Brian's original pitch, with our commentary interspersed, so you can see some of the kinds of issues that typically arise along with our suggested fixes.

Dear Erica,

Salutation is appropriate and friendly.

My agency, Essential App Marketing, is working with BolderImage to promote the release of a very exciting iPad application called iDashboard.

We felt this focus on the agency and BolderImage was misplaced. Every app better be exciting; otherwise, bloggers aren't interested. We recommend removing the intro sentence entirely. The app's price point is missing.

Not including the price in your pitch is a big error. It may give bloggers the impression that you don't think your app worth the price you're asking. Perhaps you think that making people go to the site to find out the price is some sort of enticement to get them to look at your app. (It isn't.) Always include the price upfront because it tells potential reviewers an important part of your app story.

iDashboard is a BRAND NEW iPad app that enhances your productivity by turning your iPad into a complete information center with calendar notifications, RSS newsfeeds, local weather, Facebook, Twitter, and iPod music, all on a SINGLE SCREEN!

These capitalized letters don't work well as emphasis. We'd rewrite to "iDashboard transforms your iPad into your core personal information center. View your calendar notifications, etc., all on a single screen."

As is, this text defines what the app does but doesn't motivate it. There has to be a hook sentence that personalizes the product and tells the user why they should care. Plus, more content on a SINGLE SCREEN doesn't sell the product. Here's also where a screenshot can tell the story better than the text.

Don't just charge your iPad, transform your docking time into a ONE-STOP MULTI-MEDIA INFORMATION CENTER - Keep an eye on your calendar, listen to your favorite playlist, and watch breaking news and sports. Your iDashboard is COMPLETELY CUSTOMIZABLE for your social profiles, favorite blogs, family photos, and more.

Now finally, the actual reason to be interested. Unfortunately, it's buried three paragraphs down from where it would be most effective. Ignoring the capital letters, here is the heart of the pitch—finally—and what should have started it out.

The "Don't just charge" sentence (with decap therapy) is actually a strong way to sell the app. We'd skip everything up to this paragraph except the salutation.

Erica – I've included 4 links below with more details on iDashboard:

This sounds robotic, we're afraid. We don't really care how many links follow below. We'd delete this sentence entirely and let the links speak for themselves. Plus repeating the name here ("Erica") feels second-hand-car-dealer-y: just a tad slimy and forced. We're sure that wasn't the intention, but it comes across as inappropriate.

App Link: http://itunes.apple.com/us/app/id453719557?mt=8

Press Release: http://www.idashboardapp.com/press-room/

Screenshots: http://www.idashboardapp.com/

Demo video: http://www.idashboardapp.com/demo/

If you have any questions, please contact me at [phone] or [email].

Polite and courteous contact info here, although he forgot to offer promo codes.

Thank you! -- Brian

Brian Atz, CMO, Essential App Marketing

Here, he forgot to repeat email and phone and include full contact address.

In other words, this was a pretty good pitch to begin with, but one that lost itself by burying its lede and leaving out key information.

The Rewrite

Taking all these criticisms into account, we could strengthen his pitch by condensing it and punching things up right from the start. Here's our suggestion of how a stronger pitch might read.

Dear Erica,

Don't just charge your iPad. iDashboard ($9.99) transforms your docking time into a one-stop multimedia information center. Keep an eye on your calendar, listen to your favorite playlist, and watch breaking news and sports. iDashboard is completely customizable for your social profiles, favorite blogs, family photos, and more.

App Link: http://itunes.apple.com/us/app/id453719557?mt=8

Press Release: http://www.idashboardapp.com/press-room/

Screenshots: http://www.idashboardapp.com/

Demo video: http://www.idashboardapp.com/demo/

If you have any questions, please contact me at [phone] or [email]. I'd be happy to shoot you a promo code upon request.

Thank you! -- Brian

Brian Atz, CMO, Essential App Marketing

[contact information repeated, including physical address]

Thank you, Brian, for being so kind about letting us include this!

Case Study: Remembering That the App Is the Hero

Here's a snippet from a PR agency for a recent iOS application:

I would like to inform you that (App Name) is now available on the App Store: (unlisted YouTube clip)

I'd like to invite you to take a look at our websites so you can see how powerful and feature-rich this application is (Website Link)

This pitch has several problems. The over-formal language (e.g., "I would like to") and passive voice are just the start. Every sentence in the pitch introduction (you're only seeing the first lines of a very long email) began with "I."

Remember this when pitching your apps: The hero is the app itself, not the person pitching it. There's nothing wrong with speaking in the first person, so long as you keep focus on the app and talk about what that app does.

Consider the following adaptation of this pitch:

(App Name) is now available on the App Store. See it in action here: (unlisted YouTube clip) or visit our website to explore how powerful and feature-rich this application is (Website Link)

That's not saying this is a great app pitch, but it's better than the original because the focus has moved away from the PR person who is pitching it.

Take care to avoid passive voice. Use a spell checker and grammar checker. The pitch continues:

(App name) is an evolution of the native iOS music playback application. It's simple, yet powerful interface which allows you to control, browse, list and listen to your music intuitively. (App name's) operation has a natural and ergonomic feel, which will be picked up instinctively.

Convert passive declarations (e.g., "is an evolution") into active ones. Here are a few fixes that might have helped this pitch:

(App name) evolves the iOS music playback app. Users control, browse, list, and listen to music intuitively. (App name) uses a natural, instinctive, and ergonomic GUI.

Marketing text is an art, one that relies on exciting the reader and keeping the ideas simple. When possible, try to re-edit your releases to keep these goals in mind. Here are a few pointers to keep in mind:

- Spell-check and grammar-check your release.
- Avoid passive voice.
- Make your application the hero of your write-up.
- Trim away excess text to get your point across succinctly.
- Have other people read your release before sending it out.

Case Study: The Twitter Pitch

Sending us a direct tweet isn't a great way to request a review (see Figure 5-9). That's not to say we don't respond to Twitter or engage with developers there, but there's something immediate and conversational about Twitter. Pushing into a conversation (or worse, starting one) with a pitch feels intrusive.

We prefer you to send email or to submit your requests through the normal website.

Figure 5-9
Please send email or submit your review request directly to websites.

Final Tips: Avoiding Grandiosity

Some writing habits predictably annoy bloggers. The problem is that so many words cross our desks in any day that lazy pitch writing, especially writing that employ grandiose claims, calls attention to itself via repetitive phrasing. Take time to differentiate your descriptions from the crowd and be rewarded by a more receptive audience. The following are our standard suggestions on these matters:

- **Don't overuse the word "unique."**

  If every product is "unique," none of them are. Unique means the only one of its kind. For a product to be unique, it must be singular, unlike anything else out there on the market.

  Point out features that make your product stand out and talk about how they help users rather than focusing on "uniqueness," particularly those products that are "especially unique," "extremely unique," and "the most unique."

  - We have just released this weekend a very unique app that lets you create, design and share your own moods, smileys and emoticons on your iPhone and tag people in them.

  - [Product] is an unique service that let users order exclusive, hand-drawn caricatures from their very own photo! It's a unique app, with no analogues in the App Store.

- The [Product] Stand is a unique 3-in-1 multipurpose case for the iPhone 5 with the following features.

- Available in 8 languages, [Product offers] 6 unique gameplay styles, and dozens of iconic characters in a western adventure for mobile devices like no other. Try it today!

- This is a free and unique experience as one of the best app in its category with no others in the AppStore.

· Your product is probably not "innovative."

Like "unique," "innovative" is tremendously overused in blog pitches. Innovative means a product features ideas that are new, original, and creative. Think carefully before making this claim.

Your poker game, your tip calculator, and your phone case are unlikely candidates for innovation. They may be well made, well designed, and highly functional, but ask yourself, "Are they really bringing something new to the world that hasn't been seen before?"

- I have created an innovative laptop case that uses revolutionary new materials to achieve a level of protection never before seen in a case this light and stylish.

- [Product] was born to challenge the rules of classic pen design by combining innovation, and performance to create the most inventive writing instrument.

- We are thrilled to announce our newest innovative photo/video accessory.

- This innovation is renewing one of the most famous effect of the gaming world: the parallax effect.

- I wanted to tip you to an innovative app I developed that represents a modern take on the hand turkey.

- Local multiplayer gaming is provided with an innovative pass-the-pad feature, allowing players to compete on the same device.

· Limit your superlatives.

Is your product truly a "game changer?" Is it so visionary that the entire industry will redirect itself after its debut, re-envisioning how things are done, thought about, or made? Probably not.

In a similar way, your product may not be "groundbreaking," a synonym for "innovative" or "state of the art," representing the highest level of current technology. And while many games seek to be "addicting," few actually are.

"Technically you could just take all of the superlatives, string them together in a sentence in any order and have a full PR release at your hands." – Michael Jones, TUAW

"You keep using that word. I do not think it means what you think it means." -- Inigo Montoya, *The Princess Bride*

Wrapping Up

In this chapter, we used real-life examples to point out both well-written and not-so-admirable product pitches. When you're working on your pitch, think about every phrase you write. A few things you should have learned here include the following:

- Keep it short. When a blogger has hundreds of emails to read every day, it's best to condense all the details about your product—especially the price, purpose, and unique aspects—into as few words as possible. Be pithy.

- Keep it simple. Focus on communicating in clear straightforward language instead of overwhelming us with superlatives and buzzwords.

- Show bloggers your personality. A little charm and humor can go a long way toward attracting the attention of a busy blogger.

- If English is not your native language, be sure to run your product description and pitch past a native speaker before submitting either to a blog.

6

Preparing for PR

A lot of work goes into preparing a product for its introduction to the market. Your blog pitch represents only a small part of that effort. There's a website to get ready, marketing text to create, tweets to … send, videos to produce, and more. In this chapter, we thought we'd share some of our thoughts about some of this supporting material, and how it affects us in the blogging world.

That's because, as reviewers, we experience the full gestalt of your public relations. We don't just test your product, we visit your site looking for information, we read your marketing materials, and we look at your storefronts. Your full presence on the web is just as important and interesting to us as it will be to your eventual customers. For those reasons, we decided to discuss a few critical preparation tasks that smaller devs often overlook in their run-up to product launch.

Get Your Product into Shape

This may seem like an obvious point we're about to make, but it's one that has tripped up more developers than we can count. It's this: Finish your product *before* selling it or soliciting reviews. Your product should be complete, working, and ready for sale.

Apps should be thoroughly debugged and completely tested. Hardware should be fully vetted, certified if needed, and ready to be used. Your new product should, in fact, sparkle. Submitting a product that's not ready for prime time represents an easy way to sabotage yourself and your business.

For software, your app doesn't have to create world peace, but make sure it's entirely developed and perfectly usable. Sand away any rough edges as you clean up your application to prepare it for launch. A philosophy that often hurts apps is "I'll just throw it out there and see if gets an audience." This attitude exists as a plague of half-written tech demos, partially implemented feature sets, and rushed-to-market graphics. A good application doesn't have to be overly designed. It just needs to be solid: well built, well tested, and workable.

Produce apps that do the job you state that they do, that provide enough features to make it worthwhile to its audience, and craft the app in a way that it doesn't crash or break during use. If you do that, you *will* find an audience. It's better to take a few weeks or months more to develop your app than try to rush out a product that's not ready for the spotlight. Deadlines, especially artificial ones, doom more promising apps than any other cause.

For hardware, make sure your product doesn't fall to pieces in the tester's hands (it's happened), that it does what it promises to do, and that it won't start smoking after it's been plugged in (that's also happened). If you're wait-ing on final packaging, we'll understand, but please send us materials that are fully fabricated and ready for sale.

There's a phrase that floats around the developer community, which is this: Real developers ship. We'd amend that phrase to read: Real developers ship real products. Too often, lost in the need to push an item out for sale is the understanding that the product has to offer value to the consumer and be worthy of an exchange of money. Regardless of whether your product is groundbreaking or a follow-on to an existing market, without that value, you won't receive the good reviews you're looking for and the loyal customer base your product needs.

🎙 NOTE

Although bloggers are open to beta testing participation, they typically do so as individuals because they are excited about a particular product launch, not on behalf of their weblogs. If you want a blogger to get involved early, make sure there's a compelling-enough app to support that choice. Exposing blog-gers to early buggy releases isn't always going to win support for you unless you have a strong long-range picture of where the app will eventually be. In addition, be prepared to offer bloggers just a bit more help than your other beta testers. You don't want them to get frustrated installing a beta app or understanding how it works; an early bad experience often flavors the feel-ings—good or bad—a blogger may have about an app.

Prepare Your Marketing Text

The marketing text you use to sell your product, whether on your website or on a third-party store, needs to be clear, simple, and effective. Your text explains to your customer what your product does and why they should purchase it. You need to do that without boring or confusing that audience.

Mac Developer Lyle Andrews offered some excellent advice on this in a recent TUAW interview. Here's some of what he had to say about creating marketing materials for selling your product:

Keep it short. This indicates that you are confident that the customer is going to like your product if they are interested in general. It shows you feel like you don't have to say that much to make the sale. This is true with new clients as well as products.

A long description starts to feel like an apology after awhile. However, some things are complex and merit a longer description. Conciseness is the actual metric. How can you say the most with the least words?

Keep it plain. Plain descriptions with minimal self-praise and adjectives are trusted more by App Store customers than overinflated rhetoric.

Focus on strength. Best in class in some way? Definitely say so. If nothing is the best, should you be aiming higher? This is true for Fireworks HD (http://www.tuaw.com/2011/12/27/daily-mac-app-fireworks-hd/), It Is In some ways a silly app I built to test out the store, but if you need beautiful 100% realistic HD fireworks for your event that don't repeat in sequence and work when no network connection is available, there is nothing better available for Mac than Fireworks HD.

Be a master of the obvious. While there are many great naming strategies, if you can name a product after it's product category, you have a home field advantage. With "Network Logger" (https://itunes.apple.com/us/app/network-logger/id448857637?mt=12) for instance, the genus is instantly obvious, the customer just needs to know the species. They click, they are coming to see you, you are the category. The sale is yours to lose.

Choose Strong Branding

Make sure the icon or brand that represents your product is strong and clear. For the App Store, it should differentiate itself from any other items in the same category. Don't let your look blend in with the others; make it visually distinct. And regardless of what you are selling, your branding needs to be clean, professional, and sharp.

Both customers and bloggers relate poorly to imagery that is slapdash, rushed, or appears to have been drawn by a six-year-old. A little extra investment of time or money to create a solid product image helps convey a sense of confidence in your product, that the same care was used to create it.

You can hire a company like the Icon Factory (iconfactory.com/design) to develop that branding for you—regardless of whether you're a hardware or software developer. As Figure 6-1 demonstrates, you're investing in an identity that sets your product apart from the crowd.

Abraham Vegh
Denominations – Icon Design

Developer Abraham Vegh contracted with us to create a new app icon for his currency conversion app – Denominations.

Sideric
Sensor Tools – Icon Design

Sideric tasked us with creating a unique icon that would help their first app stand out in the app store.

Strutta
Mighty Apps and Power Promotions – Icon Design

The Iconfactory created application icons to help brand two separate product suites for Strutta's social marketing platform.

Figure 6-1
The Icon Factory creates high-quality custom icons for developers.

Website Essentials

Professional product development usually implies a professionally designed website to back it up. Good websites provide product information, pricing, and sale links to where customers can purchase your product.

Your main web page should proactively offer product information to its visitors and individual product pages should inform and excite sales. Consider Figure 6-2, which shows Netwalk App's Promotee website. This page contains all the important elements needed to promote and support sales for the product. (It's also a terrific app for creating exactly the shots you need for your own professional website, so keep that in mind.)

Promotee's site offers clear branding both for the developer (Netwalk Apps) and its product (Promotee). It provides easy-to-locate purchase links both from the App Store and directly from the vendor. It explains what the product does (Overview, bottom left) and lists its key features (bottom right). And it offers support links (top-right corner) for anyone needing further information about product use before or after purchase.

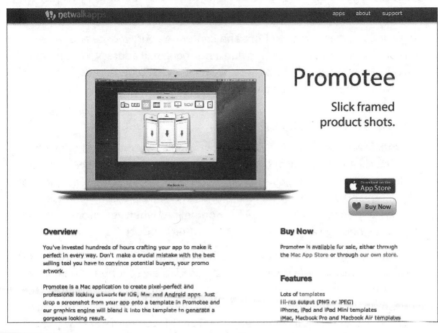

Figure 6-2
Promotee's website provides all the information potential customers need to explore the program and purchase the product.

Always make sure that your support site is ready to go before you contact bloggers for a review. Bloggers often visit product sites to check for background information, read more about the product, look at pricing, and so forth. If your website isn't live, and this isn't specifically an "advanced peek" at your app, you should not be at the point where you are sending out review requests.

If you want a professional impression, create one with a professional website.

Add a "Contact Us" Link

Make sure you put a working Contact Us link on your website. We prefer one on every page because it's much easier to find, although it's perfectly all right to place it in the "About Us" section of your site. Not all reviews happen because you submit a pitch. Bloggers often respond to word-of-mouth or come across your product through a Google search. If they cannot contact you, you lose potentially valuable coverage.

You wouldn't believe how many sites have lost these opportunities simply because bloggers couldn't figure out how to contact them. This isn't just an occasional situation; it's one that pops up frequently.

Put your contact information front and center on your website and, where possible, avoid contact forms. Provide a normal email address. We cannot tell you how many promo code requests we have messed up because it's hard to work with someone else's web page.

Take Care with Company Branding

We work in an Apple world at TUAW. Other similar websites deal primarily with Google and Android, or Microsoft or Nintendo. Apple has *very* specific guidelines for using its logos and badges on your website. The same kinds of rules often apply to other protected brands and standards, such as Bluetooth, Android, and so forth. Always check for guidelines when you promote an affiliation or technology as part of your app or other product.

With Apple, some marketing assets are strictly controlled and require marketing and advertising review. Others can be used freely so long as you follow simple guidelines. For example, here are things that make Apple cranky (see Figure 6-3): using the Apple logo, rotating Apple-provided art, and changing art colors. Other things include using the iTunes logo, animating the logo, changing logo text, and annoying passing aardvarks. (We may be kidding on the last item. Slightly.)

Figure 6-3
Apple issues strict guidelines on the use of its logos and branding.

To give you a sense of Apple's level of control for App Store marketing, Figure 6-4 reproduces their Do's and Don'ts list just for using product images on your website. This table does not even begin to cover such minutia as "Do not display Apple products smaller than 25mm in length for printed materials and 200 pixels onscreen." You can find a full marketing guidelines brochure on Apple's developer site, and we encourage you to read it through if your product is hosted on its App Store.

⊕ Do	⊖ Don't
• Use the most current Apple product images provided on the App Marketing resource site. Apple-provided images show only black products.	• Do not obscure, crop, distort, or cut off parts of the product image. Do not add or modify reflections.
• Maintain separation from other devices. Feature Apple products on their own, not grouped with products from other companies.	• Do not create buttons or icons with a product image.
	• Do not substitute white Apple products for the black product images provided by Apple.
• If multiple app screens are displayed, it is acceptable to repeat the iPad, iPhone, or iPod touch images by placing them side by side. You can place the images in either vertical or horizontal orientation. Maintain the correct relative product sizes whenever multiple products are shown.	• Do not group Apple products with competitive products.
	• Do not display an Apple product image on a cluttered background.
• Secure the display rights to any trademarks that you display on the product screen.	• Do not animate, rotate, or tilt product images.
	• Do not die-cut a printed promotion to the shape of an Apple product image.
• Display your app on the screen exactly as it appears when your app is running. Use only authentic screenshots from your app.	• Do not use graphics or images from Apple's website or the App Store. Do not imitate Apple layouts.
• Place violators, bursts, and promotional copy beside the product, not on top of it.	• Do not cover any part of the Apple product image with violators, bursts, or promotional type. Do not surround the product with a highlight.
• Use Apple product images at a size that is clearly legible at the image resolution provided. If you require high-resolution product images for large-scale promotions such as outdoor advertising, send email to appstoremarketing@apple.com and describe your marketing requirements and media.	• Do not overlap multiple Apple products.
	• Do not add cases or covers to Apple products.
	• Do not use illustration to render an Apple product, except for instructional material. If generic portable devices are illustrated, do not include details that are unique to Apple products, such as the Home button.
	• Do not use Apple product images on any disposable packaging or food industry promotions. Use the product name in text only.

Figure 6-4
Apple issues strict guidelines on the use of its logos and branding.

Creating a Reviewer's Guide

With hardware and more sophisticated or expensive apps, reviewers often receive a walkthrough or reviewer's guide from the developer. Reviewer's guides are meant for members of the media who evaluate software and hardware products. These guides explain, in a few pages, what the goal of the app is, who the intended audience is, what makes the app better than the competition, and how to use the app. If there are incredible features that a reviewer might not necessarily dig into, the reviewer's guide offers a way to highlight those features and show how to use them.

Reviewer's guides aren't huge, complicated documents. A few pages with highlights, screenshots of UI features, and some simple instructions on how to do some amazing things with the app can go a long way toward getting a reviewer excited about your product.

To get an idea of a well-done reviewer's guide, take a look at the one prepared for Penultimate for iPad (http://evernote.com/penultimate/) (see Figure 6-5). Penultimate is a note-taking app that has been acquired by Evernote. Its seven-page guide starts with a description of the app and a note about some of the glowing reviews it has received, lists its key features, and discusses the guiding principles behind the development of the app.

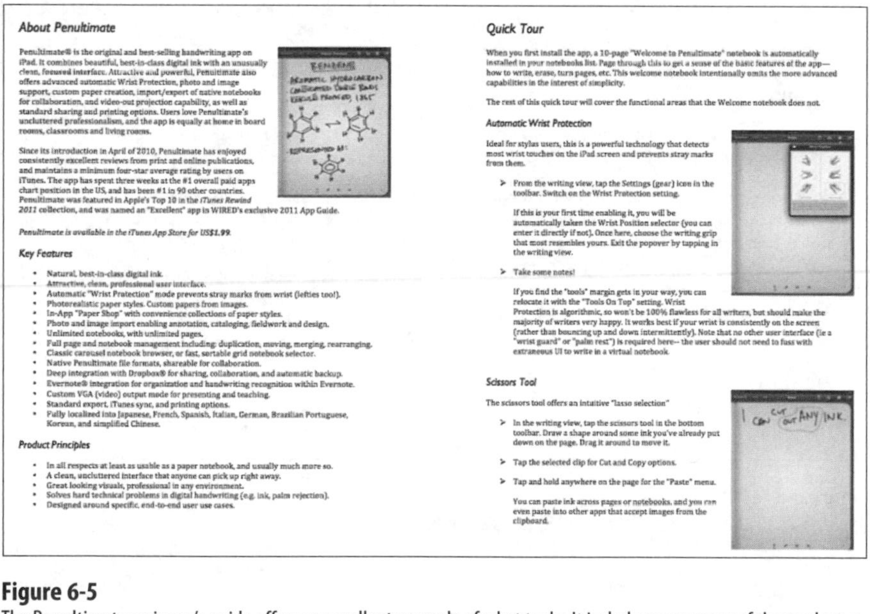

About Penultimate

Penultimate® is the original and best-selling handwriting app on iPad. It combines beautiful, best-in-class digital ink with an unusually clean, focused interface. Attractive and powerful, Penultimate also offers advanced automatic Wrist Protection, photo and image support, custom paper creation, import/export of native notebooks for collaboration, and video-out projection capability, as well as standard sharing and printing options. Users love Penultimate's uncluttered professionalism, and the app is equally at home in board rooms, classrooms and living rooms.

Since its introduction in April of 2010, Penultimate has enjoyed consistently excellent reviews from print and online publications, and maintains a minimum four-star average rating by users on iTunes. The app has spent three weeks at the #1 overall paid apps chart position in the US, and has been #1 in 90 other countries. Penultimate was featured in Apple's Top 10 in the *iTunes Rewind 2011* collection, and was named an "Excellent" app in WIRED's exclusive 2011 App Guide.

Penultimate is available in the iTunes App Store for US$1.99.

Key Features

- Natural, best-in-class digital ink.
- Attractive, clean, professional user interface.
- Automatic "Wrist Protection" mode prevents stray marks from wrist (lefties too!).
- Photorealistic paper styles. Custom papers from images.
- In-App "Paper Shop" with convenience collections of paper styles.
- Photo and image import enabling annotation, cataloging, fieldwork and design.
- Unlimited notebooks, with unlimited pages.
- Full page and notebook management including: duplication, moving, merging, rearranging.
- Classic carousel notebook browser, or fast, sortable grid notebook selector.
- Native Penultimate file formats, shareable for collaboration.
- Deep integration with Dropbox® for sharing, collaboration, and automatic backup.
- Evernote® integration for organization and handwriting recognition within Evernote.
- Custom VGA (video) output mode for presenting and teaching.
- Standard export, iTunes sync, and printing options.
- Fully localized into Japanese, French, Spanish, Italian, German, Brazilian Portuguese, Korean, and simplified Chinese.

Product Principles

- In all respects at least as usable as a paper notebook, and usually much more so.
- A clean, uncluttered interface that anyone can pick up right away.
- Great looking visuals, professional in any environment.
- Solves hard technical problems in digital handwriting (e.g. ink, palm rejection).
- Designed around specific, end-to-end user use cases.

Quick Tour

When you first install the app, a 10-page "Welcome to Penultimate" notebook is automatically installed in your notebooks list. Page through this to get a sense of the basic features of the app—how to write, erase, turn pages, etc. This welcome notebook intentionally omits the more advanced capabilities in the interest of simplicity.

The rest of this quick tour will cover the functional areas that the Welcome notebook does not.

Automatic Wrist Protection

Ideal for stylus users, this is a powerful technology that detects most wrist touches on the iPad screen and prevents stray marks from them.

➢ From the writing view, tap the Settings (gear) icon in the toolbar. Switch on the Wrist Protection setting.

If this is your first time enabling it, you will be automatically taken the Wrist Position selector (you can enter it directly if not). Once here, choose the writing grip that most resembles yours. Exit the popover by tapping in the writing view.

➢ Take some notes!

If you find the "tools" margin gets in your way, you can relocate it with the "Tools On Top" setting. Wrist Protection is algorithmic, so won't be 100% flawless for all writers, but should make the majority of writers very happy. It works best if your wrist is consistently on the screen (rather than bouncing up and down intermittently). Note that no other user interface (ie a "wrist guard" or "palm rest") is required here-- the user should not need to fuss with extraneous UI to write in a virtual notebook.

Scissors Tool

The scissors tool offers an intuitive "lasso selection"

➢ In the writing view, tap the scissors tool in the bottom toolbar. Draw a shape around some ink you've already put down on the page. Drag it around to move it.

➢ Tap the selected clip for Cut and Copy options.

➢ Tap and hold anywhere on the page for the "Paste" menu.

You can paste ink across pages or notebooks, and you can even paste into other apps that accept images from the clipboard.

Figure 6-5
The Penultimate reviewer's guide offers an excellent example of what to do. It includes a summary of the product, a key feature bullet list, and a simple tour to familiarize reviewers with the app.

Next, the guide offers a quick tour showing how to use Penultimate's built-in tools and integration with Dropbox and (of course) Evernote. At the end of the PDF document is an invitation to email the developers if reviewers have questions, with a live email link.

As you'd expect, you don't need to print out and physically snail mail this information. We've seen developers who include a PDF of information for reviewers, while others provide the URL of a website featuring text and videos highlighting the app's more dramatic features. However, if you have a physical product that you're sending for a hands-on review by a blogger, it doesn't cost any more to throw in a printed copy of the reviewer's guide.

One hardware vendor that Steve works with on a regular basis provides a folder with every review device. The folder includes a cover letter, a short reviewer's guide, a specification sheet, a business card, and one or two give-away plastic pens. It's a nice way to keep the information organized, even if the blogger isn't.

This information is generally part of a press kit that is made available to reviewers. A well-written press kit also includes information about the developers, makes comparisons with competing products, and includes contact information for reviewers who want to ask questions or get clarification on a topic. Bloggers might also need tech support, specifically if they've found a bug that somehow eluded your best testing efforts. Don't make it difficult for reviewers to contact you.

The Tao of Reviewer's Guides

Never assume that reviewers understand the function or UI of your app as well as you do. We all love our children—human, accessory, and app—in a way that cannot be matched by others. So, convey your app's functionality through a reviewer's guide. Reviewer's guides support your app by pointing out features that bloggers may otherwise overlook.

A reviewer's guide focuses on exposing features that aren't obvious and may need some manipulation to get through. We recently received a review copy of a somewhat obscure life-coaching application that focused on goal setting and problem solving. Unfortunately, despite investing time, we couldn't figure out how to use the application. We ultimately decided to give the software a pass.

This is where a reviewer's guide would have saved the review. If the developer had provided a walk-through, showing us how to set up goals, mark progress, and evaluate results, the app may have made it to our main page. Instead, it was deleted and forgotten.

A reviewer's guide typically consists of the following elements:

- Summary of your product and a list of product highlights
- Separate list of any new features introduced in this release
- System requirements list
- List of common use cases for the product
- Tutorial walk-through of the product's key features, with plenty of pictures

Think of a reviewer's guide as an opportunity to brief the press, but instead of doing it in person with a live demo, you typically provide a 5–20 page how-to document. Your goal is to move a reviewer past any hurdles in performing a hands-on inspection of your product.

Videos are never a *substitute* for a written reviewer's guide, although you can post them to the web as a *supplement*. As a rule, reviewers won't sit down and watch a long show about your product. They want to refer to a set of instructions, perform them, build a general idea of how the product works, and then start their own evaluation from there.

Reviewers don't have a lot of time to spend on each product. They need to get up and running in the shortest amount of time possible. A good reviewer's guide is short and focused. It uses a simple document layout and skips hype. Think plain text, pictures, and usage diagrams. Avoid sales pitches. You're not trying to convince anyone about your product merits, you're just trying to convey its functionality through concrete usage examples.

Remember who your audience is: people who are technically capable and familiar with normal computer operations. Leave off any "here's how you install the application or switch on the product" steps and skip directly to the "getting started" heart of your product usage tips.

Show off the highlights of your app in the fewest number of steps. If your product's features are too complicated to demonstrate in a short guide, it may not be suitable for a simple review.

🎙 **NOTE**

A quick Google search for "reviewer's guide" uncovers dozens of example documents that demonstrate real-world guides that have been issued in the past and are now archived on developer sites.

About Press Releases

For small indie developers, press releases represent pretty much the least effective way to get the word out about your product. A press release is a short written communication sent out en masse to members of the news media. You can pay a small fee to one of the many press services, and they will bulk email it to nearly every site you can imagine. You can also purchase writing services to craft a professional release.

It's a pity then that the money you pay to create and send that press release might be a complete waste. Unfortunately, many reviewers tend to skip through each morning's PR blasts. We encounter so much noise compared to so little signal in press-release content that zoning out entirely is a not uncommon response.

On the other hand, PR services such as prMac and PRWeb *can* get the word out to a number of sites that you might not even be aware of and ensure that your product gains some search-engine mojo. This helps provide you with statistics on how effective your press release was. prMac, for example, provides both free and paid press release distribution services. The extended distribution only costs $19.95 and is sent to RSS and social media aggregators, news agencies, and an extensive list of websites.

Our take is this: A well-written individual pitch to websites generally works far better in terms of connecting to bloggers than a standard press release.

In case you *do* want to go the press-release route, you can find a few excellent tutorials at prweb.com (http://service.prweb.com/learning/c/how to quick-tips) for writing press releases:

- PRWeb's Press Release Writing Fundamentals
- PRWeb's How to Write Press Releases

If you have a compelling need to create a press release, these how-to presentations offer a helpful launching pad. PRWeb also provides weekly free webinars on how to write and optimize press releases, which is helpful if you're struggling for ideas for marketing your product.

Preparing That All-Important Product Video

If a picture is worth a thousand words, then a video has to be worth at least a billion. A short, focused, and widely distributed video of the best attributes of your software or hardware product does more to whip up excitement than the rest of a well-written pitch.

A top-notch demonstration video distributed on YouTube can go viral, although it's rare, creating a tidal wave of buzz about your product that takes it from the realm of the also-rans to the hall of champions.

This section talks about some methods of capturing screen videos, what you should keep in mind when making a video, where to post the video, and how to leverage social media outlets to get views.

Recording Videos

When it comes to app demonstration, at least on iOS, one new product has solved many problems. Reflector (formerly "Reflection," reflectorapp.com) allows you to use AirPlay to mirror your iPhone or iPad screen to a Macintosh or Windows system where you can then record the screen directly from within the application.

Before Reflector, we had to either Rube Goldberg our way through creating solutions with Apple TV, video-digitizing software, and screen-capture utilities, or use an external camera to record the mobile device screen. It was a real mess, and the quality varied all over the map. This is still the case when we work with Android and Windows mobile systems.

Over-the-shoulder video is still acceptable, but try to keep things in focus (literally, although figuratively helps, too). Your camera and device should be stationary and on tripods if at all possible. IPEVO makes both the Point 2View (http://www.ipevo.com/prods/Point-2-View-USB-Camera) and Ziggi (http://www.ipevo.com/prods/IPEVO_Ziggi_USB_Document_Camera) document cameras, which ship with their own multi-jointed stands. Just place the smartphone or tablet on a flat surface, set the document camera so that it is looking down on the device screen, and then use video capture software (Apple's Photo Booth even works!) to grab your demonstration.

Don't think that you need an expensive studio video camera to shoot decent handheld demonstration videos. Many point-and-shoot cameras and even smartphones are capable of capturing high-definition 1080p video that is more than adequate to the task. Steve used a Canon point-and-shoot camera to capture an over-the-shoulder video of Realmac Software's Nik Fletcher demonstrating the wildly successful Clear app.

To shoot a product video with a smartphone, consider using a tripod mount, such as the Glif+ from Studio Neat (http://www.studioneat.com/products/glif) with a portable tripod, like the Joby Gorillapod (http://www.amazon.com/Joby-GP1-A1EN-Gorillapod-Flexible-Tripod/dp/B000EVSLRO/ref=sr_1_2?ie=UTF8&qid=1336854848&sr=8-2). An investment of about $50 provides a stable platform for grabbing video or taking high-resolution stills.

Developers of applications for Mac and Windows have many software options for capturing screencasts for product demos. Tools such as Camtasia run on both desktop platforms and capture high-quality video as you demonstrate the app on your machine. Once the video is captured, a suite of editing tools built into these screencasting apps makes it easy to do voiceovers, add titles, and even provide special effects such as highlighting the cursor or part of the screen.

Good Demo Videos Qualities

When creating pitch-ready videos, make sure you keep things short. Ideally, your video should last between 30 and 60 seconds, and always under 2 minutes. Bloggers have the attention span of fleas. Just get in there, demonstrate the heart of your product, and get out. If anyone is interested, they'll subject your product to a far more thorough look-through than any video could help with when they get a chance to test in real life.

A good product video:

- Highlights the product's core functionality through action, not just screenshots
- Showcases the product's interface and its level of finish
- Tells a story of the product's hook
- Skips the background story of the app's development (unless that story is what you're *specifically* pitching to the website)

Editing Videos

You don't need to be a professional video editor or spend thousands of dollars to make your magnum opus. Remember our discussion of the Une Bobine videos earlier in this book? Two of the three videos were made using the "film trailer" feature of iMovie for Mac; a great way to force yourself to tell your story quickly.

iMovie (see Figure 6-6) is simple enough for anyone to use, and there are similar applications available for Windows and Linux. Apple also makes iMovie for iOS, which produces surprisingly good-quality videos on an iPhone or iPad. If you've never used iMovie before, spending a few hours watching the iMovie tutorials at http://www.apple.com/support/imovie/ provides enough background to get you pointed in the right direction.

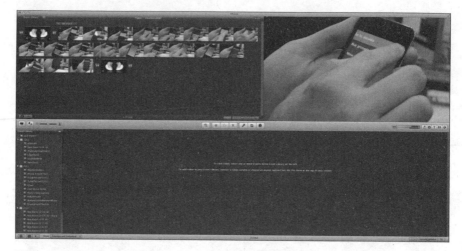

Figure 6-6
For Mac owners, iMovie provides a low-cost solution for creating high-quality product videos.

Simply capture video of your app or hardware in action, add titles where appropriate, and add music and/or a voiceover to explain important features. For the most part, letting your product tell the story is the best way to create a compelling video.

For building excitement about a product release, a series of short videos may tell the story better than one longer one. When Griffin Technology was getting ready to release its iPhone-controlled HELO TC toy helicopter, it created a trio of related videos. These told the story of a bored office worker who brought some excitement to work by buzzing his boss and co-workers with his little helicopter. Each of the first two videos provided a teaser for the next in the series, letting the story continue and resolving in the third video. Never underestimate the power of the cliffhanger ending to get viewers hooked on your videos.

Tightening Your Pitch Video

As a developer, you're well aware that selling your product is just as important as creating your product. What follows are six tips to help you create tighter video pitches. Use these suggestions to help tune your product videos before you send them off to bloggers:

1. **Be brief**—Many videos are simply too long. If your video approaches 2 minutes in length, you're forgetting a key fact about communication.
   Squirrel[1]

---

[1]   Refer to the Disney-Pixar movie *Up* for an explanation of this term.

Many busy reviewers have the attention span of a toddler, if that. Instead of spanning 2 minutes or more, try cutting your video to 30 seconds.

2. **Find your hook**—Hooks, which are the big ideas that sell your product, are often buried deep in a good video. Hooks include enticing, clever, or catchy ideas that grab a potential consumer's attention. Look for your hook, and then bring it out, punch it big time, and stop.

3. **Focus on the message**—Don't make mistake that we best characterize as "you think viewers will be as enchanted with the moment-by-moment usage of your product as you are." Don't include long app excerpts or extended moment-by-moment use of your product. Let the reviewer follow up and test the item hands-out rather than trying to engage with it as a static video playback.

   We believe hands-on testing is always a better way to appreciate a product. We don't suggest you skip product coverage entirely, mind you, but you should just offer enough to engage interest and no more. The viewer should get a sense of how the product operates, but doesn't need a blow-by-blow introduction.

4. **Communicate your successes**—Don't fail to sell a really important strength of many companies. We call this one "play your winners." If your company is rather well known for another product, we recommend that you punch that product somewhere in your presentation. If you have hired star designers or award-winning programmers, mention that.

5. **Avoid passive voice** —Drop the buzzwords and passive-voice descriptions, and offer more engaging descriptions to the viewer. More often than not, the problem stems from a "good enough" mentality. You lead with your first attempt.

   Take a break. Go back after a while and listen to your script, then edit it. You have nothing to lose but your "is"-es.

6. **Guide the viewer**—Conclude the video with concrete information of what to do next, should someone be interested in following up. It never hurts to lead a potential reviewer by the hand after engaging his interest.

Video Music

Recently, a developer sent a video as part of his TUAW product pitch. The app itself was interesting enough, but Erica was blown away by the video's music. It was smart, contemporary, and it had excellent production values. She Googled to find out more about this music and discovered AudioJungle.

We've written in the distant past about purchasing royalty-free tracks for use in products and videos, but back then, it was an expensive option with limited vendors. The track Erica fell in love with (*Give Our Dreams Their Wings to Fly* by musician Tim McMorris) cost just $14 to license in a video.

That's an amazingly reasonable price for nearly any software developer who's building a product demo reel. Instead of thinking of licensing music as an expensive obstacle, it transforms that decision into an "of course, I can afford that" mandate.

We find AudioJungle to be an incredible resource for purchasing high-quality royalty-free music and sound effects at affordable prices.

Posting Videos

You can post your video anywhere: Vimeo, YouTube, your personal website, etc. When sending in pitches, make sure you include working URLs and a description of what the video's role is (e.g., demonstration video, product marketing video, etc.).

Be sure to point out to potential reviewers if your video is capable of being embedded on a web page. Both YouTube and Vimeo provide automatic embed codes when sharing is enabled, making it simple for a blogger to add the product video to a post.

If your video is private, and not meant for public dissemination, feel free to mention that as well (e.g., "Here's a quick video demonstration of our product. Please do not share this URL with others"). On YouTube, you can disable public listing so a video can only be shared by providing its URL. That's a great option if your product or video isn't ready for prime time exposure.

At other times, however, you *will* want to create a social media push. For those situations, make it clear in your pitch communications: "Feel free to tweet about this video, whether you review the product or not." A strong, funny video can get a big jump from a Tumblr, Facebook, or Twitter mention from a large website, even if they chose not to review the product directly.

The Live Demo

During the past few years, we've seen an increase in what you could call the "live demo," a demonstration of a product done using Skype, GoToMeeting, JoinMe, and other such services. These demos take more planning to accomplish, but are a way to show off the features of your product and answer the questions of your blogger audience at the same time.

For live demos, there are some simple guidelines to follow:

- Have a real product or at least give bloggers an indication that what they're looking at is a technology demonstration and not a real product. Being shown something cool and then told after the fact that it may never make it to market can be incredibly deflating. Set expectations about the product's availability date.

- Make sure the video and sound are clear, and that you've got the technical details down before you call your first blogger. A fast way to turn off the interest of a blogger is to waste 30 minutes of her time trying to fix a sound issue during a call or showing her a barely visible demo on the screen.

- Set a time limit for the demo. Don't leave it open-ended. Let the blogger know that the demo is scheduled to run for only 10 or 15 minutes, and he'll be more likely to accept your invitation. If a blogger shows a genuine interest in you or your product, let him dictate how long he stays on the line and asks questions.

- Offer to let the blogger record the demo for a podcast. Nothing makes a video podcaster happier than to get free video content that takes up airtime.

- Follow up after the live demo. If you've promised screenshots, video links, or promo codes, send that information as soon as possible after the demo. Likewise, if you have a physical product that you're showing off and can send a review item to the blogger, do it as soon as possible after the demo to keep the blogger's interest level high. Remember that we have short attention spans!

- Thank the blogger for his time and interest, and ask if he has any additional questions.

Live demos can also be done in person if the blogger and developer are in the same city or attending the same trade show. When some of the major trade shows or expos are imminent, don't try to make an appointment with a blogger the day before or during the show. We're usually running around haphazardly and would love nothing more than to have a precise schedule of appointments to keep. Contact us well in advance, ask if we're attending the conference, and if we are, then set up a short time for a demo.

Bloggers usually enjoy meeting developers and manufacturers in person. It's a wonderful way for us to connect on a personal level, to get a better idea of the people and products we're writing about, and to even develop long-lasting business and personal relationships. TUAW Editor-in-Chief Victor Agreda, Jr., has built a continuing series of video interviews with developers known as "Origin Stories," which highlight developers and hardware manufacturers. It's a compelling video series that can give viewers insight into your product that may not otherwise be revealed.

Preparing Review Materials

When putting together review materials, you can generally focus on the basics: placing the item into the box and shipping it off to the address provided by the reviewing website or requesting a promo code or purchasing a gift card and sending that along. There are other factors to consider, however. This section runs down some of the things you may want to think about when preparing for the review.

Do You Want the Product Back?

Websites are always happy to run giveaways or donate your items to local charities. Make it clear whether or not physical products must be returned. For return items, provide a pre-addressed UPS or FedEx shipping label. Importantly, make sure *it is legible*.

That's right. We've had to struggle at the FedEx office as the clerk tried to figure out who to send the product back to because he *could not read* the form. Trying to track down a vendor to clarify an address takes time and effort, and generally irritates the bloggers who may have to spend unpaid time returning materials instead of earning money writing reviews.

Should You Include Other Items in the Package?

The rule of thumb is that you never need to include any extra items, like T-shirts, hats, basketball hoops, or other miscellanea that often accompany review items. We may give you a 3-second mention for these extra bits on TUAW TV Live, but your product receives no additional consideration or special treatment. Plus, we have to give all those items away anyway.

Should You Submit Full Copies or Time-Limited Demos?

This will sound *incredibly* self-serving, but we think you should always offer reviewers full NFR (not for retail) licenses for your products. Why? Because, a few months down the line when we're working on a write-up for a completely unrelated matter, we may think back to our original review and decide to mention it in that new post.

If we've passed the time limit for your product and can't use it anymore, you may miss out on some valuable coverage opportunities. Sure, we'll ping you again and hope to include the product in the write-up, but if the timing doesn't work out and you zig while we zag, there's a chance for good product exposure down the drain.

> 🎙 **NOTE**
>
> If you're an app developer, and specifically an Apple app developer, pick up a copy of Tokens (usetokens.com) to share and monitor promo codes. (iBookstore support has been promised for future releases.) Most Apple and Android developers should check out Promotee (netwalkapps.com) as well, which was mentioned earlier in this chapter. Promotee allows you to place screen captures into iOS, Android, and Mac hardware beauty shots for promotional purposes. These are both terrific apps for devs—well worth investigating.

Social Media

Social media outlets, like Facebook, Twitter, Google Plus, etc. (see Figure 6-7), provide excellent opportunities to extend your brand beyond a webpage. Consider creating a Facebook page dedicated to your company or product. Establish a Twitter account to be your virtual "voice." A social media strategy can help you engage with the public and promote your product.

Here are some do's and don'ts to consider as you integrate that social presence into your relationship with bloggers and customers.

Figure 6-7
Social media outlets, like Twitter, Google+, and Facebook, offer excellent ways to promote your product.

Be Interactive

Don't just post status updates. Engage in conversation. Show that there are real people behind your product and that you're there to help point people to your support pages or answer simple questions. If a blogger tweets you with a promo code request or asks for more information about your product, start a conversation. Answering a support question in a highly visible tweet is a wonderful way to show how responsive your company is to the needs of its customers.

Be Diplomatic

Don't alienate either bloggers or customers by getting into public fights, jumping into politics, or otherwise calling negative attention to your product or brand. You can use social media as a bully pulpit, but do so cautiously and with common sense. This is a business identity you're using. Remember, it's nearly impossible to retract your posts once they've gone online.

Don't Be Hostile

Don't ignore, block, ban, or argue with the public at large. This, of course, is an extension of the previous point, but it's worth repeating. Twitter and Facebook can be your ally, but if you're being hostile or rude to a customer, the world is going to see it. If you need to get into an "adult conversation" with a customer, offer to take it offline and talk to them on the phone or via email. Don't let the rest of the world see your dirty laundry.

Be Human

Bill Gerth, Comcast's PR point person on Twitter (@ComcastBill), has proved to be one of that company's most valuable assets. By providing a warm human presence, he's helped counteract a lot of the bad will aimed toward the broadcast and broadband giant.

Be Focused

Don't open your accounts to all members of your team. The voice of your brand represents you, establishing who you are and what you are to the public at large. Decide who that voice is and support that person with the time needed to create and maintain your presence.

Be Informative

Make sure the public knows when you're about to start a sale, launching a cross-promotion, or when other major developments happen. Another way to grab attention is to provide tips on using your app or product to the world at large. That's a bit harder to do in Twitter than in Facebook or other social networking apps, but you'd be surprised how much information you can get across in 140 characters.

Be Active

No one wants to "like" a page or follow a feed that's months out of date. When you commit to social media, make sure there's someone there to follow through on that promise.

Use Automatic Posting Tools

It's so easy to cross-post information on a number of social networking or web sites. Use some of the automatic posting tools that are available to do the work for you—post once on Twitter, see the post appear on Facebook, your Tumblr page, and more.

There's no reason for you to spend a lot of time updating multiple social networking outlets when there are ways to do this automatically. If your main website uses a common content management system, like WordPress, Joomla, or Drupal, any post you make can be blasted to the social networking services with no work on your part.

Cover All Possible Outlets

Sure, there are a lot of social networking sites out there, and you may be thinking that hangin' with the big dogs—Facebook and Twitter—is going to be enough. By adding other social networking outlets, such as LinkedIn, Google+, Posterous, and Tumblr, you're increasing the chance that someone is going to hear about your product. As mentioned before, many of these tools work together—one post can automatically appear on many outlets.

Be Giving

Social networking is a wonderful way to get attention by giving—giving away your product to randomly picked people who retweet or "like" a contest post. Everybody loves free software or hardware, and contests done through Twitter or Facebook are going to provide a lot of focus on your products. We suggest asking users to retweet or "like" a post to enter a giveaway; it's up to you to figure how to pick the winner.

Wrapping Up

There's more to marketing your product than just your pitch. Before you click the Send button to announce your product to your favorite blogs, be sure to have all of your proverbial ducks in a row. Those ducks should include a polished product, a good website, a product video, a reviewer's guide, and social media. Gather your flock together with these salient points:

- Don't send out information about a product that's half-baked. Bloggers and the buying public aren't happy with untested or incomplete products, so take your time and polish the product.

- Consider having a professional designer create a custom icon for your app, as strong branding can attract both bloggers and customers.

- A product video is an excellent idea, and it doesn't need to have Hollywood-caliber production values. Just make sure that it demonstrates the most valuable features of your product in as little time as possible.

- Unless your product is so intuitive to use that it needs no explanation, consider creating a reviewer's guide to lead bloggers through setup and usage.

7

The Care and Feeding of Your Blogger

Not every review is a good one. Not every reviewer loves what you have to offer. Some reviews are fair, others not so much. Your outcomes beyond those reviews often depend on how you connect with the person on the other end. Some bloggers may become great friends; others can be prickly irritants. This section discusses simple strategies you can use to respond to both good and negative coverage to help build a working relationship with your blogger.

Establishing Relationships with Bloggers

There's a basic fact of life that many aspiring product developers forget: There are real humans at the other end of your email communication. We're just as normal and flawed and needy as anyone else. If you treat us poorly, we won't react like saints. Creating and leveraging personal relationships is part and parcel of your review story.

It may seem patronizing to remind people about basic human communication when submitting review requests, but dealing with difficult high-strung personalities is a daily hassle in the blogging world.

And yes, those thorny personalities can be found on both ends of the story: developers *and* bloggers. Blogging doesn't make you a better person; it far too often transforms you into a more irritable one. Deadlines, demands, and a public ready to criticize take their toll on *both* participants in the review relationship.

Your blogger plays an important role in your product promotion story. So, what are some basics to that relationship? How do your best manage that interpersonal relationship? Here are a few suggestions to keep in mind as you start developing your connection.

Be Patient and Persistent

Bloggers always have a lot on their plate. That means the chances of your products getting lost in the mess of their commitments are higher than they might be even after a positive response to your initial pitch. This is a common occurrence, so don't take it personally.

You are your product's best advocate. Don't roll over and be weak when responding to the onslaught of a blogger's schedule and commitments. Polite persistence is a key part of that relationship.

Graciously and affirmatively promote your product, especially when a blogger loses track of you. But, do so with restraint. There's a difference between engaging in a conversation and spamming.

Touch base, check schedules, ask questions. It's expected and accepted. A developer who's too polite and unwilling to push a bit can easily get lost in the rush and tumble. Yes, a promised review or other write-up may not happen for any number of reasons, but it shouldn't happen because you're not willing to step forward and proactively support that material.

Be Understanding

Bloggers have real lives. From dental emergencies to house floods, your priorities for getting your product reviews don't always match up to the blogger's reality.

A good relationship helps you understand what's happening on the blogger's side while still advocating for your product. Remember: Human beings are a big part of this story. Be flexible and keep the conversations going. If you understand the reasons when real life intrudes, you'll find yourself in a better place to help reposition your product back into the limelight.

Accept Criticism Graciously

Some products suck and many bloggers lack tact. Always try to keep a "make lemonade out of lemons" attitude when dealing with the cretin who just publicly trashed your product on a large website in his or her thoughtless, rushed, and imbecilic review.

Part of the blogger-developer relationship involves working through these heated tension-filled moments. Stay calm and make the best out of situations you find yourself in.

"To be fair, many bloggers don't just lack tact, they downright suck."

—Jeremy Tregunna

"I wish bloggers would alert developers when they see a problem. It may not be a problem or the developer may be able to address it then and there. Please don't just blindly post about it, because then it may never get better or get fixed."

—Zachry Thayer

Advocate for Yourself

If you see issues developing, be proactive and speak up. Good, assertive resolution skills are a basis for all life relationships, not just with reviewers. Wherever you can, offer remedies and assistance. Did a review item die during testing? Send another. Is a needed server misbehaving just when a blogger is trying to use your connected app? Get the problem fixed. Bloggers expect you to be the problem solver, so make sure you're up for the job.

Products are like children. No one will ever care as much about your product as you do. Be its advocate.

Be Human

Don't spam bloggers and don't issue robotic PR dumps. A friendly human voice goes a long way in terms of conversations—and not "PR-friendly" either. Some PR flacks establish fake personalities more plastic than Barbie.

Be yourself and just try to work with bloggers on a relaxed and friendly level. Most importantly, don't be gratuitously annoying by pinging your same product over and over again. Bloggers don't want anyone to "float" something to the top of their inbox. They'd rather smash it against the wall.

Be Available

Making yourself available through phone calls, emails, and Skype can solve many problems before they become obstacles. The more flexibility with when you can be contacted, the easier it becomes for a blogger to finish covering your product successfully. We can't tell you how many times we needed instant responses to questions about sales, pricing, availability, and product shots. Having the product developer on-call meant we could finish our piece and submit it for review on time.

Be Aware of the Blogger's Focus

We can't emphasize this point enough: If a blog is focused on a specific platform or device, please don't bother us with pitches for products that are totally out of our area of interest.

At TUAW, we are focused on Apple products, so pitches for Android or Windows (at least those without some obvious Apple tie-in) fall on deaf ears. Likewise, we often hear from hardware manufacturers pitching products that are completely out of the tech realm, not just out of the Apple world. PR folks and developers who "miss the target" on a regular basis are not high on our list of favorite people.

We're well aware that many of our readers are Windows and Android users who also own Apple products. If you have a Windows app that's meant to be used with iPhones, or an Android syncing utility for OS X, we want to hear about it! Just skip the "Now available in the Android Market!" and "New for Windows Only!" catch phrases intended to excite us about that.

On a similar note, don't try to manipulate us into covering material that isn't a point of interest for our blog. We aren't going to cover a story about your product if it doesn't tie directly to our readership. Although we regularly cover the iBookstore and its associated tools, we're unlikely to do reviews on items sold there, like cookbooks or easy readers, just because, well, they're sold there. We need a story that works at a higher level, such as a biography of Steve Jobs or an iBooks Author how-to.

The "Be a Decent Human Being" Rule

One key thought to keep in mind in all of your dealings with bloggers is what is known as the Golden Rule. It's the ethic of reciprocity. Basically, treat others as you'd like others to treat you and avoid behavior that you yourself find distasteful.

Before getting angry with a blogger about a less-than-stellar review (merited or not) or pestering an unresponsive writer for the twentieth time in two days (don't laugh; it happens), step back and think about what you're doing from the viewpoint of the blogger.

Perhaps the blogger has just finished reviewing nine similar and indiscernibly different iPad cases and really didn't see what made yours so special from the rest. Maybe the blogger has been caring for a sick child or spouse and hasn't had the time or energy to pay attention to your app plea. There's possibly a very good reason why you're not receiving special treatment from your blogger.

Following the Golden Rule—or what we jokingly call the "Be a Decent Human Being" rule—goes a long way toward reducing your personal stress level and gaining the respect of the blogging world.

Let's say you're on the receiving end of what you consider to be an unfair review. Resist the temptation to blast the blogger with a nastygram. First, look for the grains of truth that might be hiding in that caustic review. Not every app or product is perfect, even if you think it is.

Next, respond pleasantly to bloggers if you choose to follow up. Don't attack the writers; they're just doing their jobs, and as human beings, they're subject to emotions, misunderstandings, and downright mistakes. Instead, ask if there's anything you might be able to discuss with them in hopes of fixing the product or app in the next revision.

Finally, keep in mind that bloggers have long memories. If your product was panned in a first version, try again after fixing any shortcomings, and then point out those specific improvements to the writer. Let him know that he's one of reasons that a revision has been made, and you're slightly more likely to get a rare "second chance" review.

Most of all, remember that there's a human being on the other end of that email or Skype call. A nice inquiry as you're developing your contact asking how the blogger is doing might give you some insight into that person's mood or current life issues.

If they're sick, in emotional distress, or just plain overloaded with work, they're probably going to let you know. Showing honest concern and care for the people who work hard to bring news of your product to the world is a great way to earn respect.

In summary, be genuinely nice, even if the blogger wasn't nice to you or your product. In return, you may just find, in time, that you have earned a vocal and supportive ally on your side.

"Kum-bai-f**king-ya"

—Anonymous Tech Blogger

Responding to Reviews—Both Good and Bad

Once a review has been published, your work has just begun. If the review was good, you now have an opportunity to leverage that review to not only promote your app and gain the goodwill of the blog that gave you the thumbs-up. On the other hand, if the review was less than complimentary about your app, and that criticism was on the mark, this is your opportunity to suck it up and take some constructive criticism.

Handling Good Reviews

When a blog gives your app a positive review, it's time to take advantage of your good fortune. Go ahead and thank the blog or blogger. Send them an email and let them know that you appreciate their kind words. Make sure that you keep the bloggers who have provided positive reviews in mind as your first contacts for future updates or new products. Grow your relationship.

Next, take advantage of the review. Use Twitter, Facebook, and your own website to let future customers know the great things bloggers said about your app. Blogs love it when you send some traffic their way by tweeting about a review they've published, and often retweet those to a greater audience (again, increasing your customer awareness).

It's also acceptable to quote the review (with proper attribution) in any promotional materials or advertisements you might send out. Bloggers are human, and like most people, they love to see their names in print. So, don't feel you only have to limit yourself to the name of the site.

Trust us—there's nothing many bloggers find more fulfilling than being quoted on a website, in a catalog, or in a product video. It's an inexpensive way to build goodwill with a specific blogger or blog that has said good things about your product.

Responding to Negative Reviews

When you receive a negative review, stop. Wait a bit before you think about responding to the blogger. If you find that most reviewers are blasting your app and focusing on the same points, there's probably some basis to their criticism. The best thing to do in this situation is to take that criticism to heart and work on fixing the issues.

Swallow your pride, and email the bloggers who trashed your app. Let them know that you'd like to resolve the issues with the app, and ask for more input. Find out what they hated about the app and have them make recommendations on what they'd change to make the app acceptable.

This is going to endear you to the bloggers, because they *always* have opinions on how apps can be better (we believe the word you're thinking of to describe them is "blowhard"), and the fact that you asked them for those opinions is going to firmly imprint you in their memories.

What you're not going to do is *change our minds*.

Even worse is the product developer who tells us in great detail why were absolutely, completely, utterly, and inexplicably deluded and wrong. And then follows up with us a few weeks or months later saying that he's fixed the product according to our recommendations and that users love the changes.

It gives us emotional whiplash, frankly.

Inconsistent Reviews

Occasionally, you may get a negative review from one or two bloggers and positive comments from everyone else. Chalk this up to a blogger who just didn't understand your app, didn't spend enough time with it, or who had a really bad hangover while reviewing the app. Yes, bloggers have bad days, too.

When a blogger makes a glaring error in his or her review of your app, definitely let him know, but be nice about it. Most bloggers are happy to correct errors or re-evaluate apps if they made an honest mistake. Being snarky to an errant blogger is not going to make you popular, so always be nice when correcting someone.

Developer Robert Jen said it best when he told us, "I don't know if this is worth anything, but I've always responded to negative reviews with a 'thank-you-for-the-recommendations-to-help-me-Improve-the-app.'"

Incorrect Facts

Bloggers sometimes get things wrong. Although we do try to check facts when possible before publication, things do fall through the cracks. You might have misspoken when we asked you for details, or "embellished" things during a phone conversation that you later regret (it happens a lot more than you might imagine). We may have copied down information from the wrong page or misunderstood details about your product. There are a lot of reasons why write-ups may need fixing.

In these circumstances, just reach out and let us know. We're nearly always happy to fix our posts after the fact, and update our write-ups with tweaks as needed.

Using Comments

Most blogs use a commenting system. This provides the best tool to respond to both reviewers and any blog readers who pan your product. Be as polite and respectful as possible.

Use facts to defend your point of view and be sure to not get into a flame war with either the reviewer or others in the comment thread. Remember: Comments are forever. They will stay attached to the review in a readable format for a long time to come.

Hi there,

I wondered if you could delete a comment I made on one of your blogs over a year ago. I am in the process of tidying up my online activity and this is one of the few posts that I am unable to remove.

Here is a link to the article, my post was posted from [personal name, URL].

Kind regards,

[Redacted]

Dear TUAW,

I am close to getting a job at Apple. I have posted a few times on this site over the years, and I'd like to remove my comments. I love this site and I'll continue to be a fan, i just dont want to take a chance that it will interfere with me getting a job. How exactly can I do this?

Thanks!

[Redacted]

For some blog readers, the comments are as much of a part of the flavor of a blog as the writing. Readers enjoy seeing or providing commentary on a post. Their feedback ranges from insightful and productive, to snarky and fight-provoking. Should you decide to take on the commenters or reviewers, you'll find that you're going to get a much more sympathetic response if you follow Robert Jen's advice and show a little humility in your dealings with other people.

Don't be hostile to the reviewer. A nasty response to a negative review is not going to endear you to the reviewer, nor is it going to improve your chances of getting reviews in the future. Be gracious, and be the bigger person. One review is a milestone in a much larger story about your company and its products.

In the same vein, don't attack others in the comments. It makes you look like a bully and reflects poorly on you, your product, and your company. Most blog commenters have a finely tuned self-importance detector and swarm when they smell an opportunity to attack.

🎙 **NOTE**

It's never wrong to disagree with a review in the comments on a post so long as you're respectful. Be polite and don't get defensive.

Why Wasn't My Product Reviewed?

Nothing can be more frustrating than sending a promo code to a blogger who obviously has an interest in your app, but then never follows up with a review. Other times, you've made your best pitch to a blog and still don't get any love. Why didn't they review your product?

There are a lot of new apps announced every day, but for each blog, there is only a finite number of bloggers who all have a limited amount of time to write. Even great apps may be overlooked, so don't be upset if one of the big blogs ignores your work.

As noted earlier in this book, many bloggers write about certain areas that they specialize in. One blogger might know navigation apps, another may have expertise in music apps, while a third is the game app writer. Your app might be released at the same time that the specialty blogger is out of the country, having surgery, or busy at his or her "real job."

Here are some reasons your app might not have made it to the front page:

- **So many apps, so little time**—With a limited number of post slots per day, bloggers often have to pick from a number of shiny choices for which apps get the review coverage. If your request arrives in a flurry of app releases, it has to fight for those slots.

- **Right app, wrong staffing**—The right person might not have been around. Is yours a weather app, a navigation app, or an education app? Many bloggers specialize in particular areas, and other writers on that site defer to the expert. If your review request arrives when the specialist is on vacation or traveling, it may get lost before he or she returns.

- **A little goes a long way**—Even those apps we like, we have to balance. Sometimes, there's too much of a good thing. If two high-quality photo apps arrive at once, we may pick one over the other rather than trying to cram both into a single review.

- **There's only so much room**—A good app, a good pitch might not make the cut. Although bad pitches are easy to pass over, good pitches aren't guaranteed a review slot either. It's not just because you did a poor pitch. It's just the reality of the situation, our time limits, post limits, and so forth.

- **This town ain't big enough for two nearly-identical apps**—Sometimes, the strangest coincidences happen and we receive two or more product pitches for similar apps at the same time. Your app may not necessarily at the top of the review heap in that case. However, many bloggers try to give your app the benefit of the doubt in a case like this by adding links to similar apps.

One of the key things to keep in mind is this: It's almost *never* personal. Your product wasn't skipped because the blog doesn't like you. More likely, it was a mix of timing, staffing, and space.

You are your product's champion. Be polite and persistent.

Wrapping Up

As with most things in life, marketing your product through blogs is all about relationships. Starting off on the right foot and remaining civil in all of your communications with bloggers can pay off with long-term relationships that give your products an edge in getting coverage.

When thinking about the human factor in creating those relationships, here are some points to ponder:

- Be a decent human being. This is The Golden Rule, and it should be foremost in your mind when you're communicating with a blogger. To be honest with you, some bloggers obviously don't have this in mind when they respond to you. Be better than them, and stay nice.

- Take negative reviews as feedback on how to improve your product. Sure, sometimes, the review can be painful and result in lost sales. If you show that you can improve your product by viewing the review as constructive criticism, you may impress the same blogger who originally took issue.

- Especially for new app developers or small manufacturers, remember that you're a small fish in a vast sea. Don't give up if your product is overlooked for a review from a major blog. Just keep up your good work and, eventually, it should pay off.

8

Worksheets and Checklists

Throughout this book, you've read about ways you can evaluate and improve your pitches. You've read about the way online websites work and how to position your product for the best possible outcome. To help support your efforts, we developed a series of worksheets and checklists.

As Apollo's temple of Delphi states, "know thyself." These items help you assess your product and potential customers as you prepare to enter the marketplace. When completing these forms, don't fool yourself or "best case" every scenario. Be as honest with yourself as you can.

If you don't know an answer to a question, do some online research and then make an educated guess. Your answers might not necessarily be exact, but at least by looking into a particular area, you are covering some bases you may not have considered before.

Know Your Customer: Developing a Customer Profile

Before trying to sell customers on a product, consider how large your potential customer base is and whom your product targets. Are you writing an app for pregnant women who use an Android 4.0 device? That's a much smaller potential market than a game app based on a popular movie that runs on all mobile and desktop platforms.

We don't want to move you away from a small audience if you can potentially capture the market with a must-have item. If you make a few tens of thousands sales at a good price in a small market, that may carry your company just as well as an ad-supported app with a million installs.

Before you start selling, you need to know who is out there, why they'll want your product, and the likelihood that you can reach that audience through sales. So, your first job is to describe what the product is and who it's aimed at.

Worksheet 1: Likely Customer Overview

Ask yourself the following questions:

- Who is going to purchase this product?
- What problem does your product solve? What does your product *do* for the customer?
- Who has this problem or need?
- Describe your typical customer in detail, including age, gender, job title, likely income, and interests.
- What skill level and technical experience does your customer need to use your product?
- What are the important demographics about your customers that would influence the utility of your product and their likelihood of purchase?
- About how many people fit this customer profile in the world?
- Why, specifically, would your customer *need* this product?
- Why, specifically, would your customer *want* this product?
- Do customer geography, culture, and language play a role in this product? If so, how?
- What system requirements (hardware, software, etc.) does your product require from your customer?
- What is your expected price point for the product, and how much pain does this involve for the customer? Is it an impulsive buy or something that requires comparative shopping? Is your customer relatively affluent?
- What special-interest groups does your product target? How do you describe these groups? Will a customer self-identify as a member?
- Why should the customer purchase *your* product instead of competing ones?
- Of those people who might buy your product, which customers are valuable and which ones are not? Does your product provide a natural loyalty and upgrade path? If so, describe the customer qualities that influence a continued revenue stream.

Competitive Analysis

One measure of potential success or failure in the marketplace is your competition. It doesn't take a lot of hard thinking to realize that, if you come up with a product that is virtually identical in form and function to many other products, there isn't a compelling reason for someone to choose a new entrant into the market.

In this worksheet, we want you to evaluate your potential competition. Unless you've developed something completely different than has ever been created before (we doubt it), you *will* have competitors.

For *each* competitive product, fill in the blanks as best you can. The idea here is to identify who your competitors are, their strengths and weaknesses, and how your product compares.

This is an incredibly important task for you to undertake, because it gives you an indication of whether or not your product really has what it takes to grab market share from competitors. It may also point out whether your app or product will even make a splash in the market if it is a poorly thought-out "me too" attempt at cashing in on a trend or fad. Remember, this is most useful when you do your research and complete this for every potential competitor.

Worksheet 2: Evaluating Competition

Ask yourself the following questions:

- What is the competing product name?
- How much does it sell for?
- What regions of the world does it sell in?
- Does it provide any differentiating features in those regions (e.g., language support, voltage support, etc.)?
- Is price higher/lower than my product's expected price? How does it compare in price on a per-unit basis?
- What features does the product have that yours does not?
- What features does your product have that this competitor does not?
- What are the strengths of this product?
- What are its weaknesses?
- What is the overall word of mouth on this product? How does it perform in online reviews, customer reviews, and other assessments?
- What is its approximate market share?

- How visible is this product in the marketplace? How did it gain that visibility?
- What does its good reviews point toward in terms of features and functions?
- What does its bad reviews focus on?
- How is it marketing this product?

Potential Market Size Calculation

Reality check time.

We know of way too many app and accessory developers who don't put a lot of time and effort into thinking about the potential market size for their product. As a result, they often believe that they will sell millions of units and become despondent when the actual number is in the hundreds.

What we're going to do here is work through a simple calculation based on what we call the shrinking circle effect (see Figure 8-1). To start off, determine the total platform size for your product. This is constantly changing, but a quick Google search can provide you with reasonably accurate numbers, especially if you're publishing for iOS, Android, OS X, or Windows.

For example, say that you're developing an iOS app. The most recent accurate numbers we found while updating this book were from September 2012. That's when Apple announced that it had sold 400 million iOS devices. In the best possible case, all of those devices are being used by someone, somewhere. In reality, many are broken, have non-working batteries, and were either recycled or thrown out. However, start by assuming the best-case number—400 million in this example.

Next, think about the percentage of that platform that meets your system requirements. Say that your product uses some features that are only found on the iPhone 5. That considerably shrinks your market. Some online articles by Wall Street analysts point to iPhone 5 sales in the range of 45 million worldwide in the three months ending December 31, 2012. Sales during September were estimated at around 10 million for an estimate of 55 million iPhone 5s. That's a much smaller number than 400 million. Your potential market just shrank.

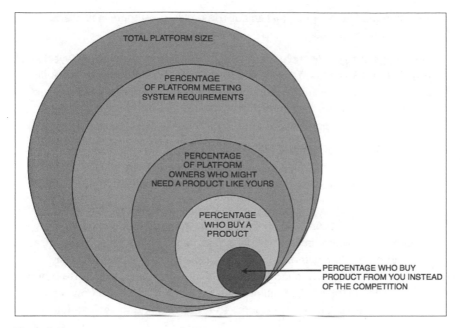

Figure 8-1
Shrinking circle effect.

Next, think about the percentage of that body of iPhone 5 users who need or want your app. This is where the estimating can get way off. It is best to assume the worst possible case as a result. Imagine an early K-through-3 educational game app aimed at American boys in the 5-to-9-year-old range. A quick look at Wolfram Alpha (http://wolframalpha.com) reveals a current population of 10.2 million boys in that age range. But, how many of those kids have access to an iPhone 5?

Again, it's educated guess time. Almost a year ago, about 91.4 million smartphones existed in the U.S., meaning that about a third of the population now owns one. That means that about 3.4 million boys have access to a smartphone. If iPhones account for 40 percent of that number, our market drops even further to .4 x 3.4 million = 1.36 million. If iPhone 5s are only about a third of all iPhones in the U.S., that number drops down to about 452,000.

Not every 5-to-9-year-old boy in the U.S. with access to an iPhone 5 will want to play your game. Educational games are a bit like software broccoli or spinach. They don't appeal to everyone. It's time to perhaps do a little market research. Maybe you get a sampling of kids in that range and see how many of them really like your app. Out of 20 boys in the age range, maybe half are enthralled with it, while the other half start playing Angry Birds Star Wars almost immediately. Now, you can cut the previous estimate in half, and you're down to 256,000.

This brings us to the next barrier to entry: What percentage of 5-to-9-year-old boys in the U.S. can talk a parent into installing a kid's game onto an adult's iPhone 5? It's an educational game, so you've got a bit of a sales advantage there in talking down the parent. Kids can be persistent, but many parents would probably respond with a stern "No!," even with a tutorial title.

Let's say that 80% of all those adults decide that they don't want little Johnny's sticky fingers on their new iPhone 5, but 20% are already thinking about their next phone purchase, so they agree to buy it. Multiply 256,000 by .2 and you're now down to 51,200 or so units.

Finally, think about competition to your app. Perhaps your competition is other games that are similar. After all, educational games are going to attract more attention from parents of 5-to-9-year-old boys. If your app is really unique, the competition might be minimal. But, if the app is similar to others, a likely scenario for a K–3 edugame, you might want to see just how many competitors are out there and assume that you're going to get an equal slice of the pie.

As an example, if there are three other similar games aimed at the same potential market and your app is the fourth entrant into the market, expect that you're going to get one-quarter of that market at best. A little math shows that you're down to .25 x 51,600 = 12,800 units.

When we talk with developers about estimating market share, we tell them to run both best-case and worst-case scenarios. That will at least give you a range of answers, and the high end will hopefully keep you from getting too frustrated about continuing development.

When budgeting for promotion of your product, keep in mind the lowest sales number. That way, you won't be tempted to overspend and potentially lose all of your profits. If sales are actually higher, you'll have a nice bonus coming your way.

Be sure to think about some other things when working on a budget. If you charge $0.99 for each copy of your app, you'll make about $0.69 on each sale after Apple takes its share. That number may vary with other App Stores or distribution methods, but be sure to take that into account. Here, our mythical 12,800 units might make us about $8,832; not a big number, and it probably won't come all at once.

Pretty rough news to take, isn't it? You can overcome that low-earning potential through creating "insanely great" apps that meet a need that nobody else is addressing for a wide audience of potential buyers, and of course, marketing can increase your sales (although at a cost).

No single market-size calculation is going to be completely accurate, because the inaccuracies inherent in each one of our estimates are multiplied with each calculation. Remember, this is just providing an educated guess at what your potential market size may be; it's not a precise accounting of exactly what your sales will be.

Worksheet 3: Market Size Calculation Worksheet

Use Table 8-1 to help you estimate the size of the market for your app.

Table 8-1   Market Size Calculation Worksheet

Market Size Estimate	Best Case	Worst Case
[A] Total platform size		
[B] % of devices meeting system requirements		
[C] % of device owners with a need for your product		
[D] % of device owners who will potentially buy product		
[E] % who buy your product rather than the competition		
Market size (units)		
Likely sales: (A x B x C x D x E)		

Pitch Checklists

Your product is built, you're ready to ship, and it's time to put together your pitch. Before you click the Send button on your email application to send that all-important pitch email, run its subject line through this first checklist to give your email a better fighting chance of actually being read by a blogger.

Remember that the subject line is the first thing a potential reviewer sees. Unless you start selling from that very first element, chances are poor that anyone will open your email and keep reading the rest of your pitch. Here's what you need to check.

Worksheet 4: Checking Your Subject Line

Check that you have done the following:

- Included a subject line in my pitch email.
- Included the product name in the subject line.
- Checked that the product name is spelled correctly.
- Explained what the product does.
- Left out a request in the subject line to have my product reviewed (it is implied).
- Included the platform(s) the product works with.
- Included a motivational hook for the product to capture the reader's attention.
- Explained who the product is for and what genre it belongs to.
- Considered or included a timely tie-in or promotion.
- Made sure the subject line is as short as it can possibly be.

After you review your subject line, turn your attention to the contents of your pitch. You need to make sure that you hit all the standard points each pitch should contain. The next worksheet helps you review your pitch to make sure that you haven't forgotten any of the core elements needed by reviewers to properly process your request.

Worksheet 5: Checking Your Pitch

Ask yourself the following questions:

- Does your pitch include the exact name of your product, what it does, and why it is different?
- Have you remembered to mention the price you will charge, including the monetary units (for example, dollars or Euros)?
- Did you add links? Always include a link to your product page on your site and another to its ecommerce product page (e.g., on iTunes, Google Play, Amazon, etc.).
- Are there one or two screenshots or glossy product shots?
- Did you provide a link to a short video showcasing the product?
- Is there a concise description that specifies the audience, what the app does, and what sets it apart from the crowd?
- Did you remember to provide contact information? Include an email address, any phone numbers, and optionally, Skype and Twitter IDs.

Reviewer's Guide Checklist

Remember that a reviewer's guide can help your product gain extra exposure if the reviewer can become intimately familiar with the key features of your product in a short amount of time. Here is a checklist of things to include and omit in your reviewer's guide.

Worksheet 6: Essential Reviewer's Guide Elements

Check that you have done the following:

- Included a summary of my product.
- Included a list of product highlights.
- Included a list of new features introduced in this release.
- Included a list of system requirements.
- Included a list of common use cases for my product.
- Wrote a step-by-step tutorial walk-through of the product's key features.
- Included many screenshots in my tutorial.
- Omitted sales pitches in my reviewer's guide (not required).
- Omitted installation or startup instructions. (It's implied that the reviewer will know how.)

Blogger Relationship Database

It's a good idea to think about setting up a blogger relationship database so that you have a list of contacts to work with for your next successful product.

Worksheet 7: Blogger Contact Details

Here are some example fields that you may want to include when capturing this information for your target blogs and bloggers:

- Blogger first and last name.
- Blogger nickname.
- Blogger email address.
- Blogger telephone number (if provided).
- Blogger shipping address (if provided).
- Blog name.
- Blog URL.
- Specific title at blog (if any).

- Blogger's "beat" or interest.
- Does the blogger have a podcast? If so, what's the name, schedule, and media (audio or video)?
- Past reviews of products similar to mine (provide links).
- Past reviews of my products (if any, provide links).
- Last contact with blogger (when and where ([if you met in person]).
- Summary to use in the future when reminding blogger of previous contact.

Wrapping Up

This chapter provided you with some tools to use before you begin work on your product, during your marketing work, and in the future when contacting bloggers about new products. As you work on perfecting your pitch, use these worksheets and checklists to hone your marketing skills:

- Know who your customer is by developing a detailed customer profile.
- Are you entering a saturated market? A competitive analysis helps you decide if you have a chance at capturing a significant market share or just the scraps that are left.
- Perform a potential market size calculation to see if your product development work is really going to be worth the effort.
- Fine-tune your pitch and reviewer's guide by using the appropriate checklists from this chapter.
- A blogger contact database is worth considering if you're in the market for the long haul.

Index

Q

R

Safari
Books Online

FREE
Online Edition

Pitch Perfect
The Art of Promoting
Your App on the Web

"A must-read for anyone trying to get their app reviewed by the media."
—Aaron Watkins, President, Appency PR

Your purchase of *Pitch Perfect* includes access to a free online edition for 45 days through the **Safari Books Online** subscription service. Nearly every Addison-Wesley Professional book is available online through **Safari Books Online**, along with thousands of books and videos from publishers such as Cisco Press, Exam Cram, IBM Press, O'Reilly Media, Prentice Hall, Que, Sams and VMware Press.

Safari Books Online is a digital library providing searchable, on-demand access to thousands of technology, digital media, and professional development books and videos from leading publishers. With one monthly or yearly subscription price, you get unlimited access to learning tools and information on topics including mobile app and software development, tips and tricks on using your favorite gadgets, networking, project management, graphic design, and much more.

Activate your FREE Online Edition at
informit.com/safarifree

STEP 1: Enter the coupon code: OFHNOGA.

STEP 2: New Safari users, complete the brief registration form.
Safari subscribers, just log in.

If you have difficulty registering on Safari or accessing the online edition,
please e-mail customer-service@safaribooksonline.com